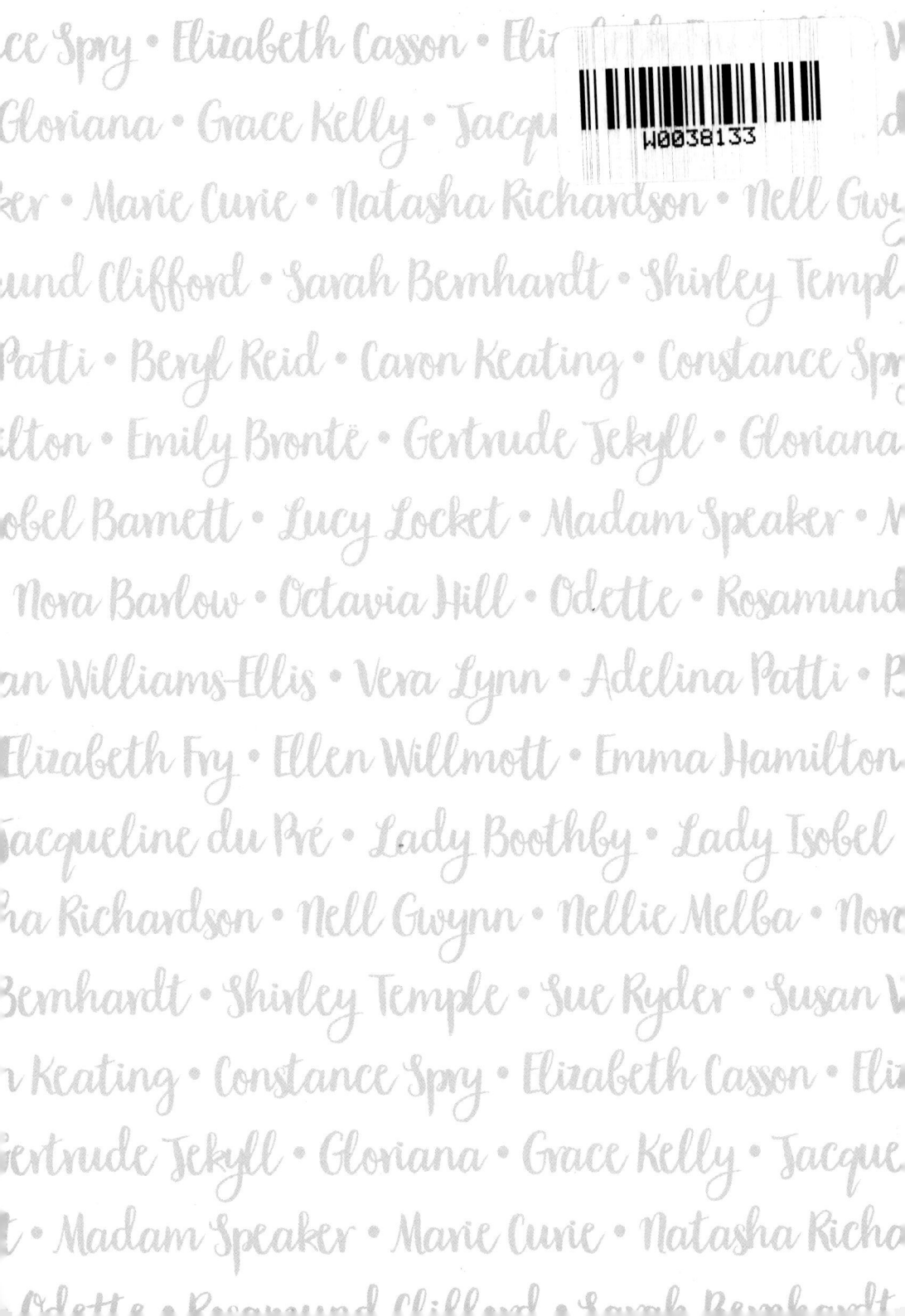

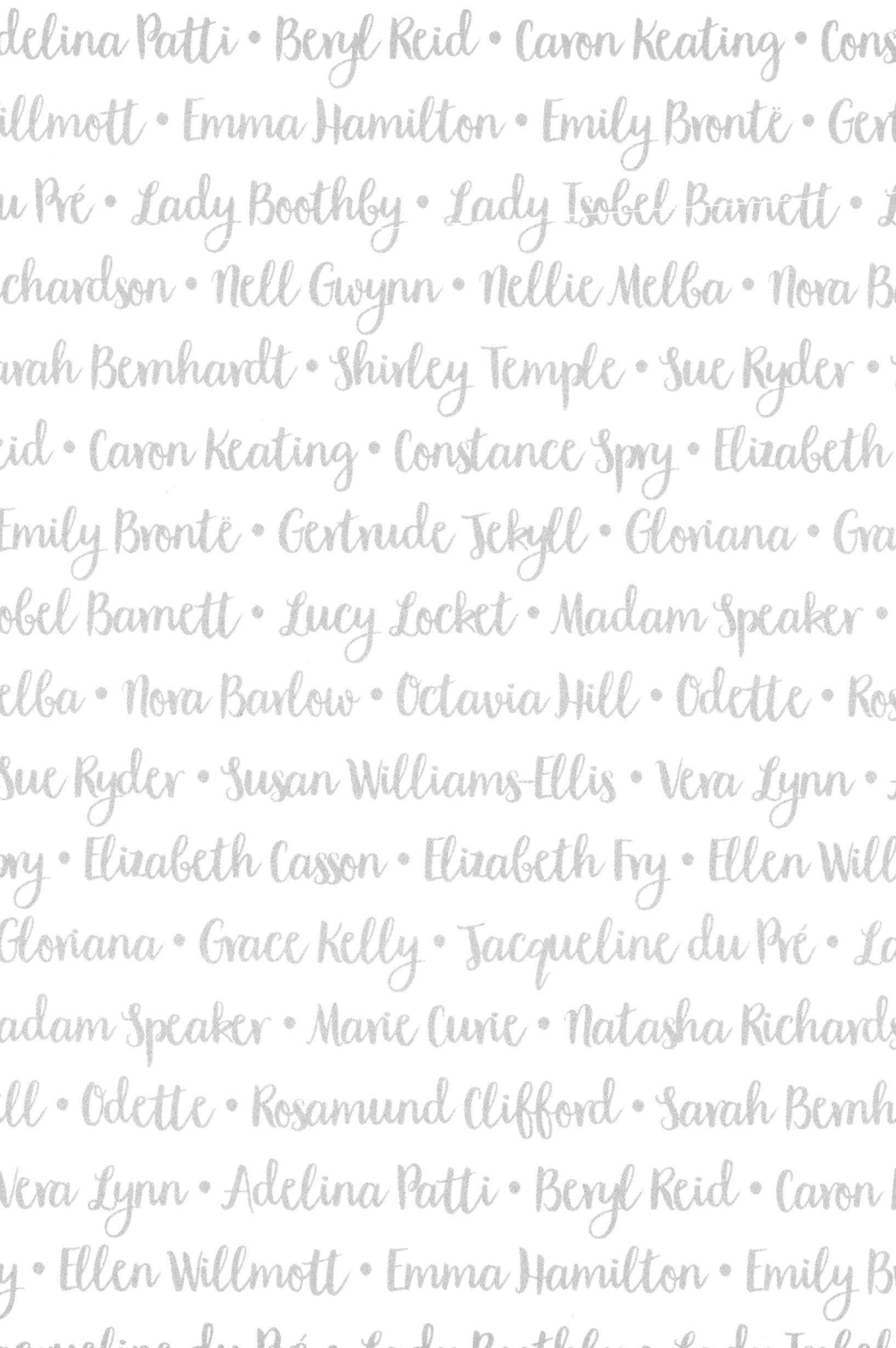

Thirty remarkable women and the flowers named after them

Pretty Maids

Mari Griffith

Foreword by Alan Titchmarsh

GRAFFEG

Pretty Maids
Published in Great Britain in 2019
by Graffeg Limited.

Written by Mari Griffith copyright © 2019.
Designed and produced by Graffeg Limited
copyright © 2019.

Graffeg Limited, 24 Stradey Park Business
Centre, Mwrwg Road, Llangennech, Llanelli,
Carmarthenshire SA14 8YP Wales UK
Tel 01554 824000 www.graffeg.com

ISBN 9781912213856

1 2 3 4 5 6 7 8 9

Contents

The Pretty Maids

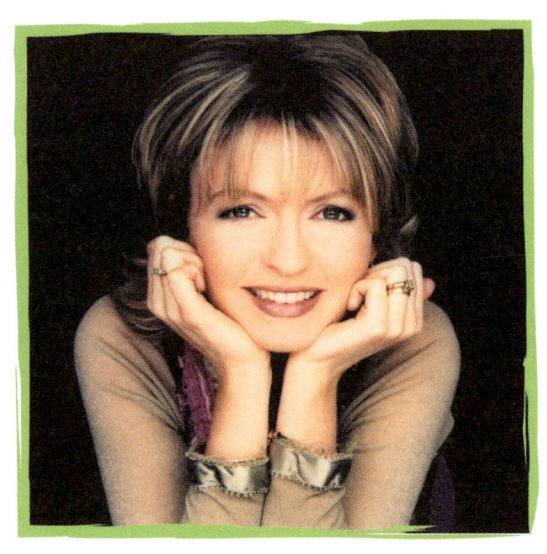

In support of
THE CARON KEATING
FOUNDATION

THE MARIE CURIE FOUNDATION

MACMILLAN CANCER SUPPORT

Mary, Mary, quite contrary,
How does your garden grow?
With silver bells and cockle shells
and

Pretty Maids all in a Row

This popular nursery rhyme has been sung by children for hundreds of years and no one can be exactly sure whether the 'Mary' of the title refers to Queen Mary I of England, Mary, Queen of Scots or perhaps even the Virgin Mary. Whoever 'Mary' was, it's certain that this seemingly innocent little song disguises references to violence, aggression, political upheaval or religious persecution. We won't celebrate any of that!

Instead, let's take a closer look at the lives of some of the remarkable women who have been paid the exquisite, fragrant compliment of having flowers named in their honour.

These are the 'Pretty Maids' featured in this book. Come into our 'garden' to meet them, to learn a little more about them and the reasons why they inspired so much admiration, not only in plantsmen but in everyone whose lives they touched.

Mari Griffith

Alan Titchmarsh

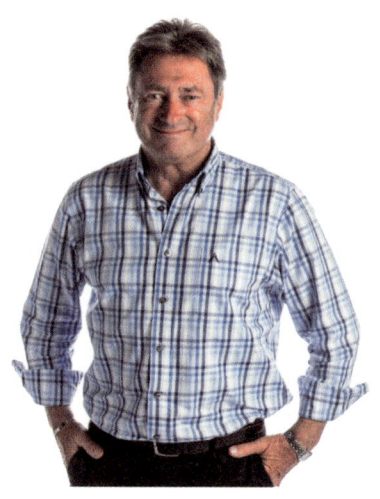

This book is an unashamed celebration of beauty, particularly the beauty of flowers, and that will always appeal to me as a gardener. What appeals to me as a man is that it also celebrates the kind of beauty which sets some women apart. I don't mean the airbrushed artificiality of the glossy magazine or the cat walk. I mean the kind of beauty which lights up the eyes, which animates the countenance with the joy of living or smiles out from the face of compassion: the kind of beauty which makes plantsmen want to name the flowers they have grown after the inspirational women they admire.

This book is dedicated to the memory of just such a young woman, Caron Keating, known and loved by millions of television viewers as the presenter of many popular programmes. I first worked with Caron's mother, Gloria Hunniford, in 1988 when we co-hosted the gardening programme *House in a Garden* on BBC Radio 2 and, even though I think I got to know Gloria quite well, I cannot imagine how devastated she must have felt when she learned that her beautiful, vital child had been diagnosed with breast cancer. It is to Gloria's great credit that, after her daughter's death, her way of assuaging her profound grief was to set up a charity in Caron's name which would help others who were going through the same pain and heartache. In the intervening years, the Caron Keating Foundation has raised several million pounds, all of which has gone to help other cancer sufferers and their families. Gloria was proud to be awarded an OBE in the Queen's Birthday Honours list in 2017 for her services to cancer charities.

One of the many imaginative ways in which the Foundation raises money is through the sale of the Caron Keating rose, a delightful, fresh-scented floribunda in a gentle tone of glowing apricot. Developed and grown by the Harkness nursery, it was introduced in 2006, two years after Caron's death and the foundation benefits from 10% of the net catalogue sale price of each bush. By buying this book you, too, are contributing towards this valuable resource because a percentage of the proceeds from the sale of it will also benefit the Foundation.

As you stroll through our virtual garden, you might decide that you'd like to grow some of these lovely flowers for yourself, so contact details for the specialist nurseries and societies are

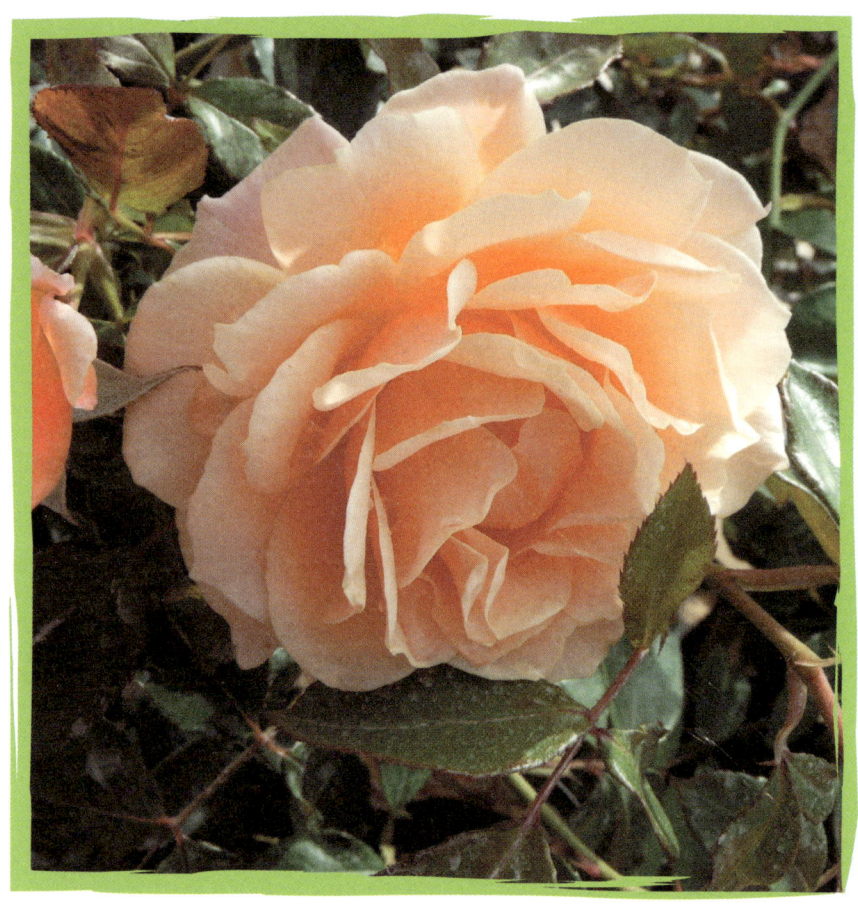

Rose 'Caron Keating'

included, along with tips on how to get the most from your flowers. The growers and specialist plant societies have been very keen to help with this project and we would sincerely like to thank them all.

Have you ever stopped to wonder who names the flowers? And how? Or, indeed, how you might set about having a flower named in honour of someone whom you hold in high esteem? Well, the naming of plants is a very precise procedure and often bewildering to the layman so we're grateful to the Royal Horticultural Society for allowing us to demystify the process with the adaptation of an article from their website, explaining how to set about it. That appears on page 196.

So, come, allow me introduce you. No doubt you will already be familiar with some of these wonderful women but you're sure to be meeting others for the first time. Here they are, from Adelina Patti and Vera Lynn to Elizabeth Casson and Sue Ryder: there are some whose names might have been largely forgotten had they not lived on in the names of flowers. The bouquet which you will find within these pages contains thirty of the loveliest 'pretty maids' of all and I promise you that they will never fade. And they are bound to bring you pleasure because flowers, as John Ruskin put it, seem intended for the solace of ordinary humanity.

Alan Titchmarsh

The Caron Keating
Foundation

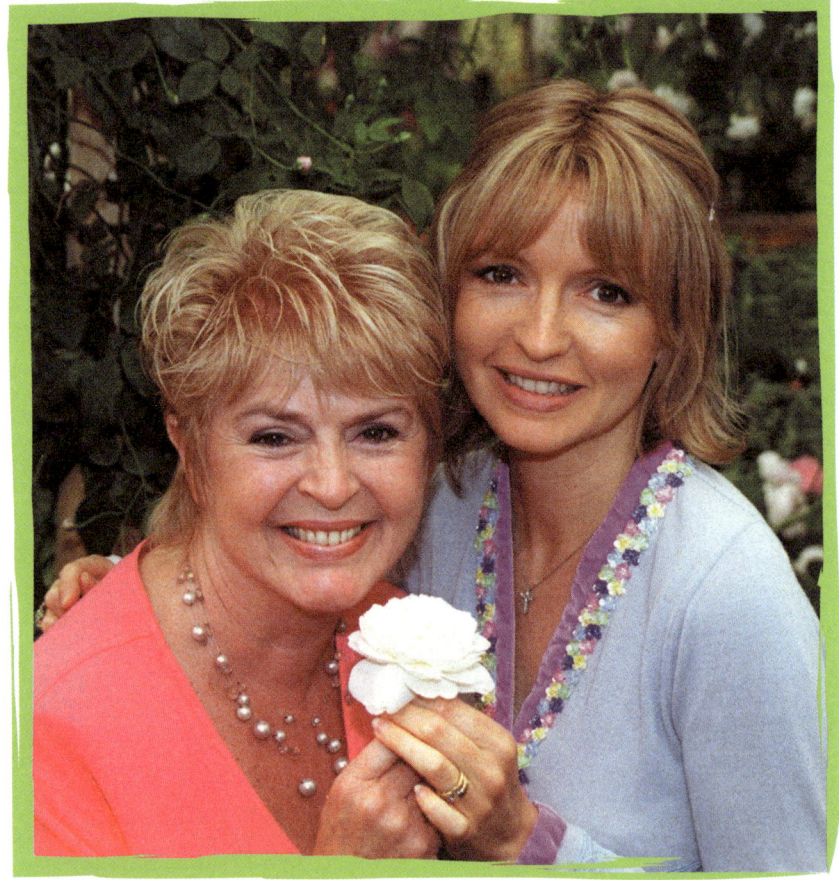

Mother and daughter together in May 2000.

My daughter Caron was first diagnosed with breast cancer in 1997 when she was in her mid-thirties. At that time she was a much-loved young television personality, having presented programmes such as *Blue Peter*, *This Morning*, *Top of the Pops* and *Entertainment Today*. She was happily married with two young sons, Charlie and Gabriel. After her diagnosis, she spent the next seven years valiantly fighting and managing the disease through a range of orthodox and complimentary cancer treatments. The support she received during that time was second to none. Caron learnt so much about the disease during her tenacious, worldwide search for knowledge, as did I and all the other members of our family. Sadly, Caron lost her battle in 2004 and subsequently the family set up The Caron Keating Foundation, which now gives grants to all types of cancer charities in her name. It seems that cancer has touched most people in the UK, through the experiences of friends, colleagues and family, and it has become a disease that no one can afford to ignore. Statistically, one in three of us will be diagnosed with cancer at some stage in our lives. According to Cancer Research UK, breast cancer is the most common cancer among women with more than 55,000 new cases diagnosed annually, claiming around 11,000 lives each year. More frightening statistics show that every day, over 900 people in the UK are told they have some form of cancer.

But it's not all bad news. With the advent of earlier detection and improved treatment and drugs, cancer death rates in the UK have fallen dramatically in the last ten years, and this trend will hopefully continue. I used to work with Mari Griffith in Northern Ireland on a television series called *Talkabout*, way back when Caron was a little girl. Though we both remained in the broadcasting business, Mari and I went our separate ways and hadn't seen each other since then but when she wrote to me out of the blue to say that she'd had the idea for this book and would like to work on it with me for the benefit of the Foundation, I was very pleased to pick up the threads of an old friendship. The book is Mari's way of saying 'thank you' to all those who helped her during her own experience of the disease.

The Caron Keating Foundation makes a considerable difference to many individuals and families affected by cancer. It targets and financially assists small but significant cancer charities, professional carers and support groups. It is a family-run Foundation which I set up after my daughter's death with the help of my sons, Paul and Michael, Caron's brothers. I am its Administrator and the Foundation's only cost is one part-time secretary, with all the money raised going to cancer charities across the country. You can learn more about the Foundation, its aims and its achievements by visiting the website at www.caronkeating.org (Registered Charity 1106160)

Some of the profits from the sale of this book will go towards enabling the Foundation to continue its work but, just as Caron would have liked, it will also give you, the reader, the pleasure of getting to know a little bit more about some of the wonderful women throughout history who have had this very special tribute paid to them. Their names will live forever in the beauty and fragrance of flowers.

Gloria Hunniford OBE

Adelina Patti • Beryl Reid • Caron Keating • Cons
Willmott • Emma Hamilton • Emily Brontë • Ger
du Pré • Lady Boothby • Lady Isobel Barnett • L
Richardson • Nell Gwynn • Nellie Melba • Nora B
Sarah Bernhardt • Shirley Temple • Sue Ryder • S
Reid • Caron Keating • Constance Spry • Elizabeth
• Emily Brontë • Gertrude Jekyll • Gloriana • Gra
Isobel Barnett • Lucy Locket • Madam Speaker •
Melba • Nora Barlow • Octavia Hill • Odette • Ros
• Sue Ryder • Susan Williams-Ellis • Vera Lynn • S
Spry • Elizabeth Casson • Elizabeth Fry • Ellen Will
• Gloriana • Grace Kelly • Jacqueline du Pré • La
Madam Speaker • Marie Curie • Natasha Richards
Hill • Odette • Rosamund Clifford • Sarah Bernh
• Vera Lynn • Adelina Patti • Beryl Reid • Caron
ry • Ellen Willmott • Emma Hamilton • Emily B

Now, come and
meet the 'maids'

CAMELLIA JAPONICA
'ADELINA PATTI'

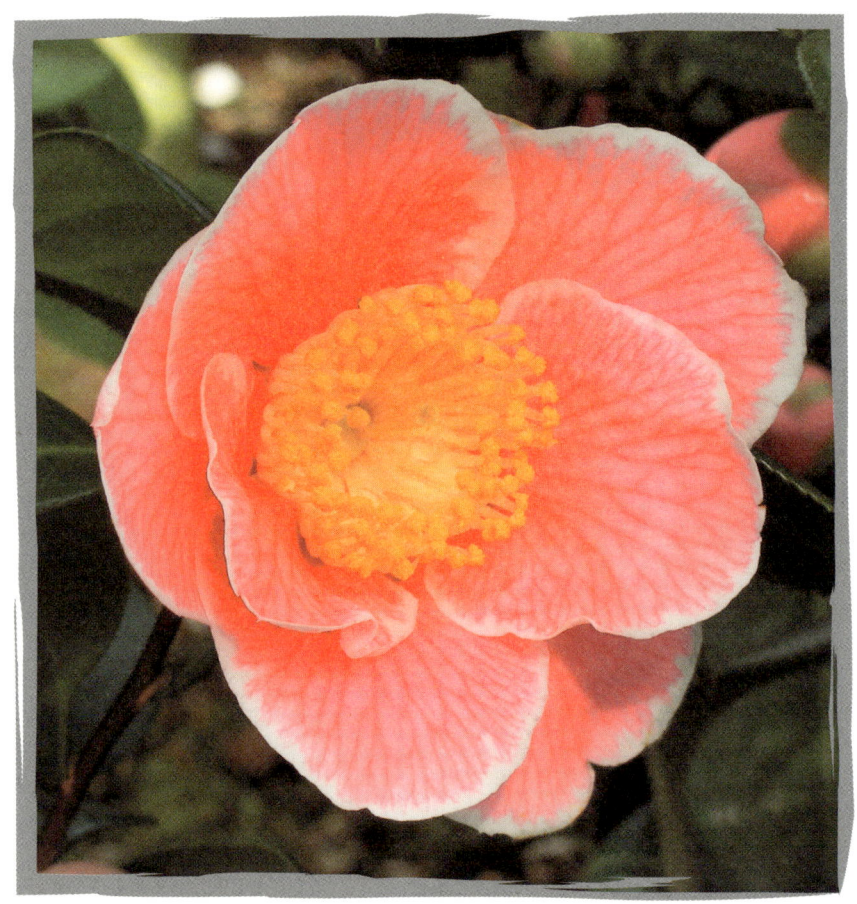

© Trehane Nursery

Adelina Patti

1843–1919

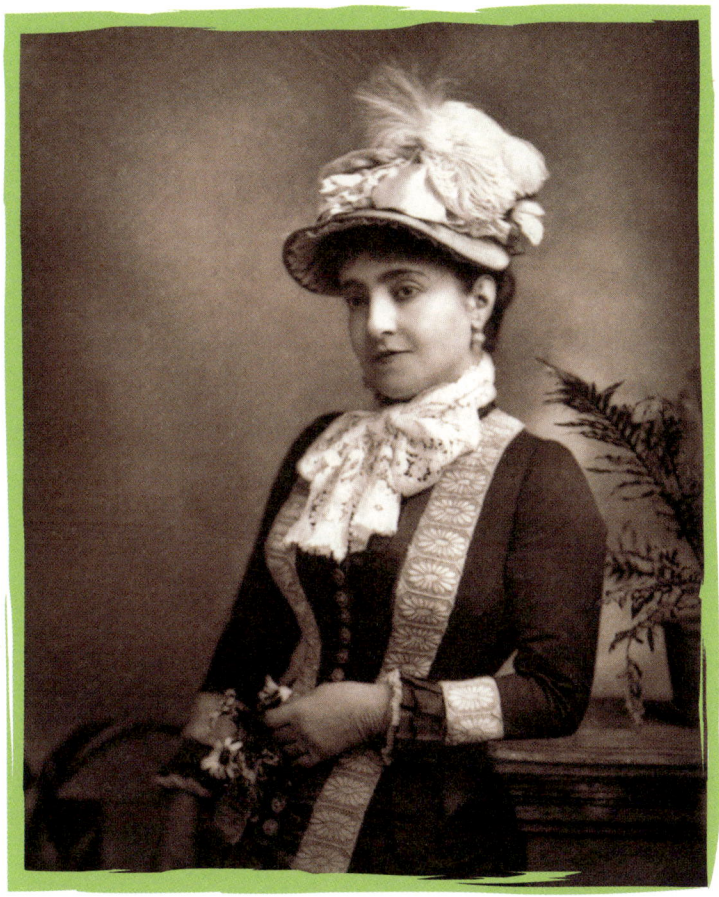

When asked to name his three favourite opera singers, the
composer Rossini replied 'Patti, Patti and Patti'.
Quite a commendation!

CAMELLIA JAPONICA
'ADELINA PATTI'
IN YOUR GARDEN

This camellia species occurs naturally across south-eastern Asia, particularly in Japan, where it was often grown in temple gardens.

First imported to the UK in the early 1800s, camellias have been popular ever since and 'Adelina Patti' is one of the most attractive and rewarding of the many varieties available.

It should be planted in ericaceous compost in partial shade and is perfectly happy in a large container, particularly if given a little protection in the worst winter weather.

Fully hardy throughout the UK, it does nevertheless benefit from a little shelter in the far north. With an erect growing habit and pendulous branches, it produces bright rosy pink single flowers, broadly banded white on the margin and with golden yellow anthers, blooming over a period of four to six weeks between February and April.

Container-grown plants benefit from regular pruning, which also encourages new growth. There is advice on every aspect of camellia cultivation on the Trehane Nursery website.

Trehane Nursery, Stapehill Road, Wimbourne, Dorset, BH21 7ND. Tel: 01202 873490. Email: office@trehanenursery.co.uk. www.trehanenursery.co.uk. See also: The International Camellia Society. www.internationalcamellia.org.

Adelina Patti

Queen Victoria's favourite singer, the soprano Adelina Patti was the first true diva, a superstar of the operatic circuit, a beautiful woman who possessed a remarkable voice of such purity and flexibility that it thrilled her devoted fans in Britain, the United States, Europe, South America and Russia. At the pinnacle of her career in the late nineteenth century, she commanded a huge fee of $5,000 for every appearance and remains one of the most famous sopranos in history. The Italian composer Guiseppe Verdi went even further and said she was perhaps the finest singer who had ever lived. Tsar Alexander II of Russia awarded her the Russian Order of Merit in 1870.

Her parents were both opera singers, so it was quite natural that the young Adelina should follow in their footsteps. Her first appearance was at the age of 16 in 1859, when she sang the title role in Donizetti's *Lucia di Lammermoor* in New York. Two years later she starred in Bellini's *La Sonnambula* at Covent Garden to great acclaim and enjoyed being in London so much that she bought a house in the city and used it as the base for her international career. She travelled extensively and it was in Washington in 1862 that she sang *Home, Sweet Home* for President Lincoln and his wife, Mary, both of whom were moved to tears by the sheer beauty of her singing.

The song became associated with Patti for the rest of her life and she would often sing it as an encore to please her cheering audiences at the end of a performance.

Adelina Juana Maria Patti was a truly international celebrity; born in Spain of Italian parents, she was brought up in New York and carried a French passport, having been married for the first time to a French husband. That marriage ended in an acrimonious divorce which cost Patti half her considerable wealth, but she had already found the great love of her life, the tenor Ernesto Nicolini. Of necessity, theirs was a clandestine romance and in 1878 Patti purchased a castle in Wales where the lovebirds could live in luxury, away from prying eyes. This was Craig-y-Nos (which means 'Rock of the Night') and it became very much more than a love nest: it was Patti's cherished home for the remainder of her life. She spent a fortune on it, adding a clock tower, two turreted wings and a large greenhouse, filled with exotic plants and birds. She and Nicolini were eventually married in 1886 and they threw open their wonderful castle home to friends from all over the world, among them several of the crowned heads of Europe. Patti extended the castle yet again and had a small, acoustically perfect theatre built there, where she gave frequent recitals. The theatre, an international opera house in miniature, still exists. Nicolini died in 1888 and, in 1899, Patti married for the third time. Her husband was the handsome Swedish aristocrat Baron Rolf Cederström, who was nearly thirty years her junior. The couple continued to live at Craig-y-Nos until Patti's death.

At the height of her fame, Adelina Patti's voice was without equal but it went unrecorded, of course. However, she did make some early recordings during 1905 and 1906 for what was then the Gramophone and Typewriter Company of London. Recording techniques were rudimentary, she was now sixty-three years old and the voice had deteriorated with age, so the recording gives us no real indication of the sparkling performances which had thrilled thousands.

Her last public appearance was at London's Albert Hall in October 1914, when she sang for the benefit of the Red Cross and their work at the front in the First World War. She died in 1919, a year after the war had ended.

PELARGONIUM
'BERYL REID'

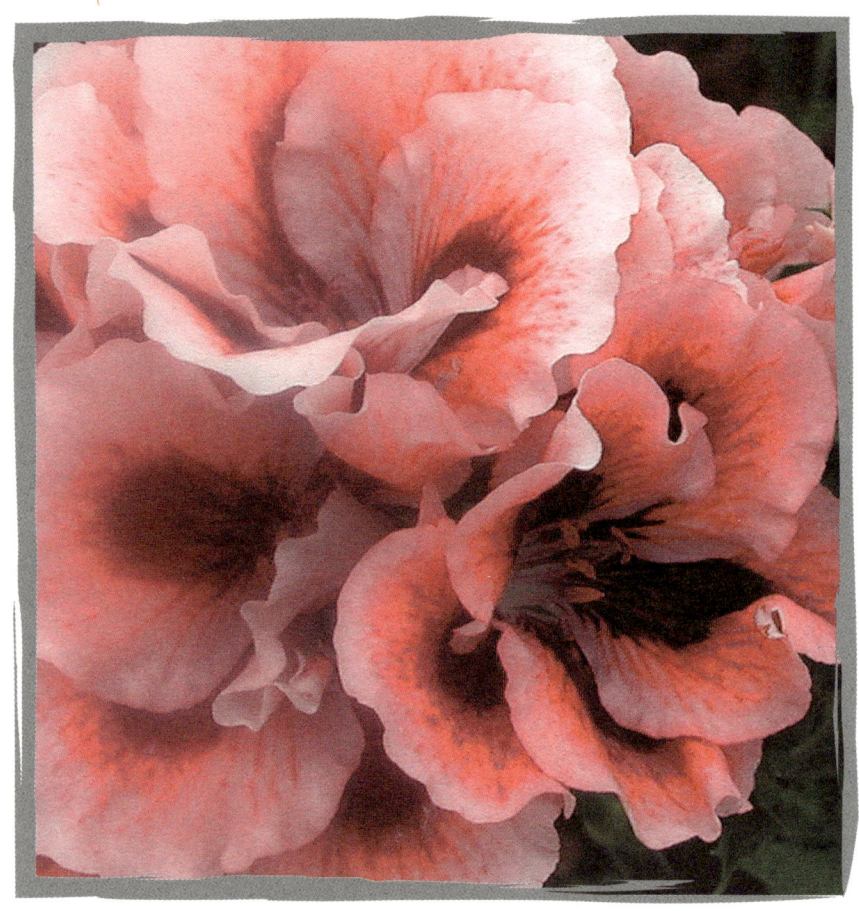

© Fibrex Nurseries Ltd

Beryl Reid

1919–1996

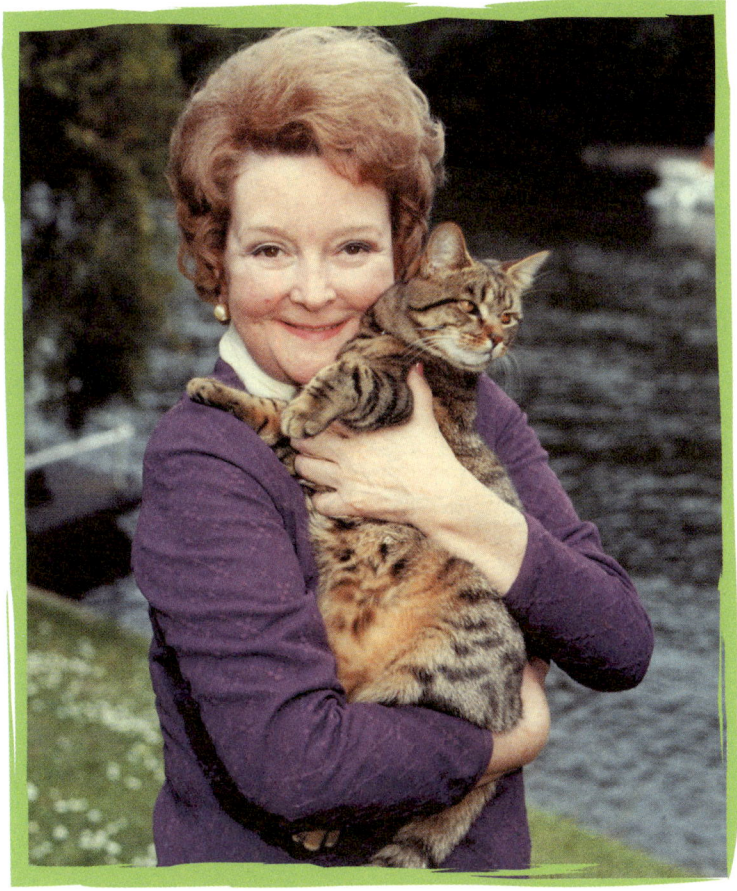

Beryl in the garden at Honeypot Cottage, with one of her much-loved cats. Photograph by Allan Warren.

PELARGONIUM
'BERYL REID'
IN YOUR GARDEN

The large peach flowers of this regal pelargonium have a burgundy blaze on the upper petals, making the compact, bushy plant a great companion for either reds or pinks and blues in a patio display.

Pelargoniums are not hardy so they are best grown in tubs, pots or planters in sun to part shade in a soil-based compost.

Water fairly sparingly since they dislike being water-logged but will reward a weekly liquid high potash feed by producing an impressive display of flowers all summer long, from May to September.

They can be overwintered in a heated green house or conservatory. Strip off the leaves to aid ventilation and keep the plant quite dry.

It's a good idea to prune them lightly at this time, taking about a third off and using these cuttings to produce new plants for next year. The parent plant should be re-potted in the spring with fresh compost.

Fibrex Nurseries Ltd, Honeybourne Road, Pebworth, Stratford-upon-Avon, CV37 8XP. Tel: 01789 720788. Email: sales@fibrex.co.uk. www.fibrex.co.uk. See also: The Pelargonium & Geranium Society. www.thepags.org.uk.

Beryl Reid

Beryl Reid was one of Britain's best-loved actresses, with a fine line in comedy. Born in Hereford of Scottish parents, she later moved with her family to Manchester.

Beryl began dancing lessons at the age of three and perhaps this influenced her later techniques as an actress. She said she always approached a new role by getting the physical attributes of a character right, from the feet up – even when she was working on radio! Initially, her father had serious doubts about his daughter's ambitions to become an actress and she was first employed behind the counter of Kendal Milne's department store in Manchester. But within a short time she had joined a concert party and was touring and appearing in pantomime and summer seasons all over the country. During the war years, she entertained British armed forces personnel as a member of ENSA, the Entertainments National Service Association, along with several artists and actors who found fame before and after the war years, including Gracie Fields, Joyce Grenfell and Laurence Olivier.

Beryl's radio breakthrough came in 1946 when she appeared on *Henry Hall's Guest Night* in the character of Monica, a wicked, posh-voiced schoolgirl with quotable catchphrases which immediately caught the imagination of the audience. She went on to feature among the regular cast in *Educating Archie* as her most enduringly popular character, Marlene, a tough dancehall raver with a Brummie accent. She rapidly became a national institution, a radio monologuist with a huge loyal audience who wouldn't miss any programme in which she appeared.

By now a major star, she made frequent guest appearances on stage as well as on radio and her comic gifts were much in demand. This led her to attempt to achieve her real ambition to try 'legitimate' acting and her West End debut was in *The Killing of Sister George*, playing June 'George' Buckridge, a hard-drinking lesbian soap actress. It was a daring part in a daring play but her performance was highly acclaimed and when it transferred to New York it won her a Tony award in 1967. But the UK tour of the play was not a success and Beryl was puzzled by the reaction she met in the general public. They associated her so much with the character she portrayed that they cut her dead in shops and refused to serve her. Even so, when the play transferred to film in 1968, Beryl won a nomination for a Golden Globe Award for Best Actress in a Motion Picture Drama.

Beryl was an actress, pure and simple. She had never wanted to be anything else. On screen, she scored another huge hit in the film of Joe Orton's *Entertaining Mr. Sloane* in 1969, then went on to appear on stage in several roles, including the Nurse in *Romeo and Juliet* with the Royal Shakespeare Company. On television, towards the end of her career, she made an extraordinary impact in the role of Connie Sachs alongside Alec Guinness in the screen adaptation of John le Carré's *Tinker, Tailor, Soldier, Spy*. She went on to take the BAFTA Award for Best Actress when she subsequently appeared in Le Carré's *Smiley's People*. Her health, though, was beginning to let her down and she had been diagnosed with osteoarthritis which caused her considerable pain, making it much harder to work. For the first time in her life, she was forced to cancel appearances.

Beryl is still remembered with great affection as an exceptionally talented and intelligent woman who hated any kind of pretension. Naturally funny, gentle and generous, she nevertheless didn't take her success for granted, to the point of being something of a workaholic. In fact, her biographer, Kaye Crawford, claims that she never took more than three holidays in the whole of her 60-year career! Perhaps her personal life suffered as a result of this single-mindedness because, though she married twice, neither marriage lasted. She spent her final years living alone at Honeypot Cottage, her eccentric riverside home in Buckinghamshire, with her many cats.

BUSH ROSE
'CARON KEATING'

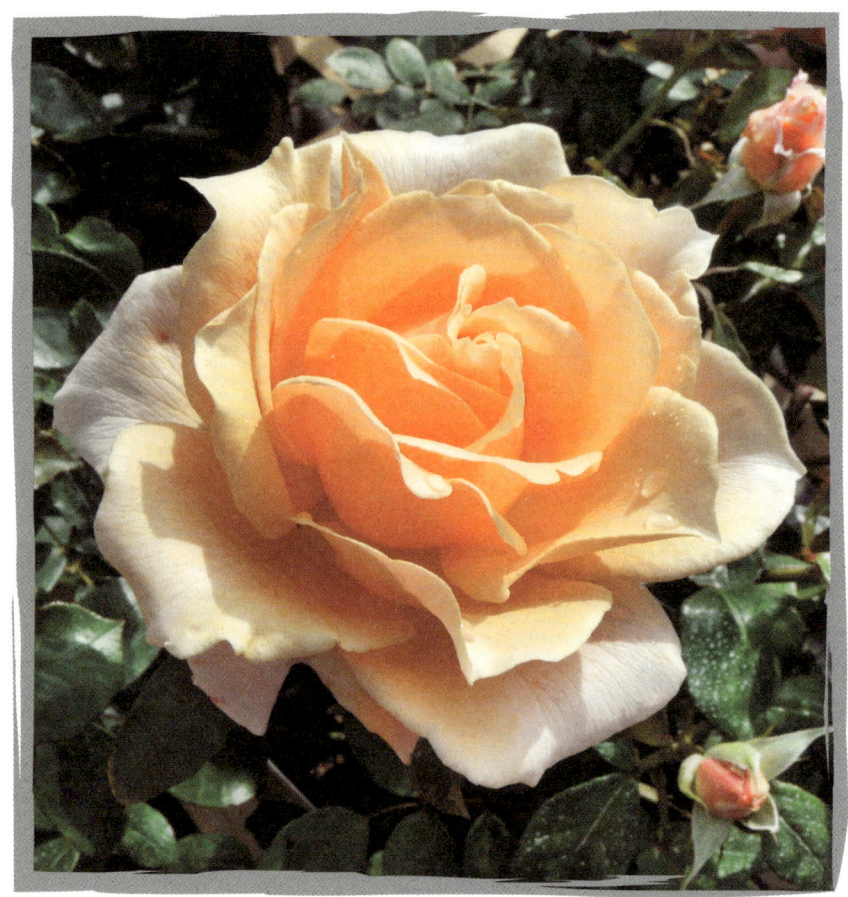

© Harkness Roses

Caron Keating

1962-2004

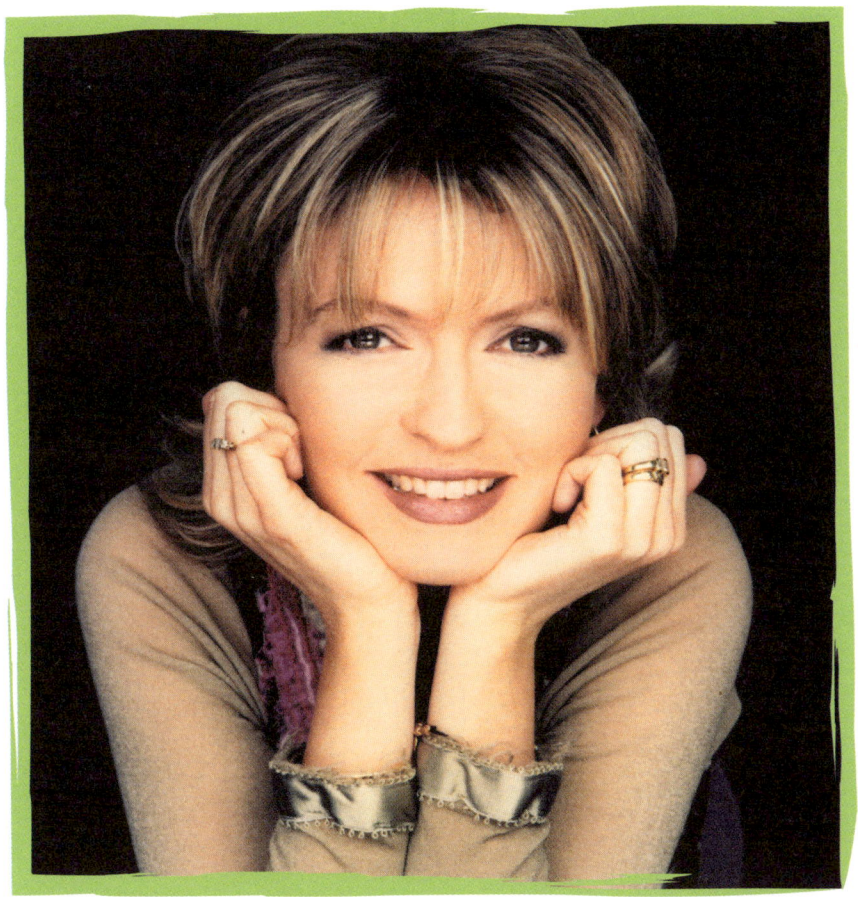

Caron at the height of her fame, the busy young television professional
with everything to live for.

BUSH ROSE
'CARON KEATING'
IN YOUR GARDEN

Appropriately enough, 'Caron Keating' is one of the Harkness Nursery's five-star-rated floribunda roses with a perfume rating of four. With five to seven flowers per cluster and a colour range which fluctuates between a warm, gentle pastel shade of peachy pink through to a glowing apricot, it makes a truly outstanding border rose.

After the rounded bush has provided a multitude of blooms, which emerge from delicate buds in early to mid-June, it can be relied upon to give a repeat performance again in late summer, treating the gardener to a flowering spectacle twice in one growing season.

The mature bush will reach 90cm tall x 80cm wide (approx. 3ft x 2.5ft) and its rounded shape makes it a particularly good rose for planting in groups, though it is equally happy in beds or borders. The added bonus is that it is also wonderful as a cut flower.

Harkness Roses, Cambridge Road, Hitchin, Herts, SG4 0JT.
Tel: 01462 420402. Email: harkness@roses.co.uk. www.roses.co.uk.
See also: The British Association of Rose Breeders. www.rosesuk.com.

Caron Keating

Born in Fulham, London, but brought up in her native Northern Ireland, Caron Louisa Keating was destined for a career in television. Her parents, BBC producer Don Keating and presenter Gloria Hunniford were both broadcast professionals and Caron's degree from Bristol University was an Honours BA in English and Drama. Sure enough, after a spell of presenting in Belfast, her infectious humour, attractive personality and professionalism landed her the dream job of presenting the BBC television flagship children's series *Blue Peter*. Caron was game for anything on the show from interviewing Prime Minister Margaret Thatcher in the studio to undertaking some daring exploits on film including jumping under freezing waterfalls, diving with sharks and abseiling down cliffs and skyscrapers. A naturally pretty girl, Caron always managed to look good whatever she was doing, but she was often wearing clothes she had found in charity shops. Charming, funny, articulate and spirited, Caron Keating became a huge hit with the viewers and an effective role model for an army of young fans.

Caron stayed with *Blue Peter* for four years before moving on to present a number of high-profile programmes for an adult audience in several different genres, proving her great versatility. She took current affairs and consumer programmes in her stride, as well as *Top of the Pops*. She reported from the

Olympics in Barcelona, hosted her own radio magazine show for BBC Radio 5 and co-presented the extremely successful *Schofield's Quest* with Phillip Schofield before being signed up as the Entertainment Correspondent on the highly successful News Network programme *London Tonight*. She was also a fine young actress and her work included a starring role in the drama production *Finbar's Class* in Northern Ireland. On the BBC1 network she presented the four-part documentary series *Routes and Rhythms* which examined the association of music and religion.

Marriage and motherhood meant taking time out from broadcasting and Caron was immensely proud of her two sons, Charlie, born in 1994 and Gabriel, born in 1996.

She returned to our screens in 1998 to present the top daytime programme *This Morning* and the ITV prime-time consumer show *We Can Work It Out*. It seemed she had a charmed life but there was a dark cloud on the horizon. By now she had been diagnosed with breast cancer and took a sabbatical because of it, spending time with her family at her home in Fowey, Cornwall, returning to television only briefly to present the prime time entertainment programme *Rich and Famous* for ITV.

Her health was not improving so, in a bid to beat the disease with complementary medicine and a different lifestyle in the sun, Caron moved to Byron Bay, Australia in December 2001, with her husband Russ Lindsay and their children, but she was slowly losing her brave battle against cancer. She came back to the UK three years later and died peacefully at her mother's home in Kent on 13th April 2004. She was just forty-one years old.

After Caron's death, her mother and two brothers, Paul and Michael Keating, set up the Caron Keating Foundation in her memory. A fund-raising partnership, the foundation offers financial support to professional carers, complementary healing practitioners and support groups as well as individuals and families who are affected by the disease.

Gloria Hunniford later charted her daughter's courageous journey through the disease in a personal and very moving book entitled *Next to You*. One of the many warm reviews which greeted its publication praised Gloria's extraordinary honesty in writing it, adding that 'both Caron and Gloria come across as amazingly strong, loving and inspiring characters.'

ENGLISH CLIMBING ROSE
'CONSTANCE SPRY'

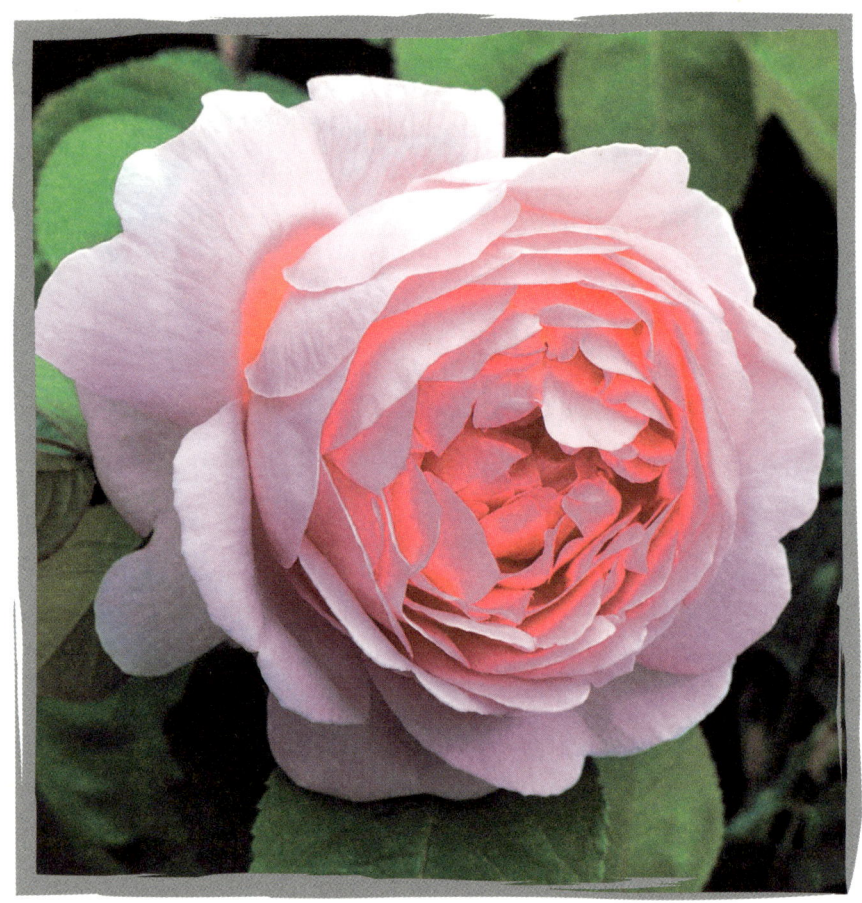

© David Austin Roses

Constance Spry

1886–1960

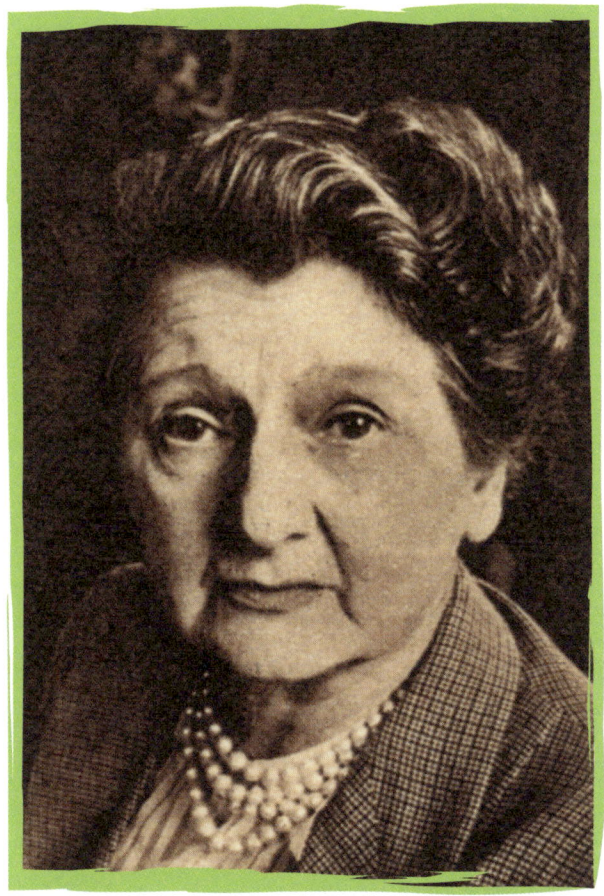

The doyenne of flower-arrangers, remembered in her
favourite flower.

ENGLISH CLIMBING ROSE
'CONSTANCE SPRY'
IN YOUR GARDEN

The original English climbing rose from the David Austin nursery, 'Constance Spry' produces magnificent, deeply-cupped, pure mid-pink blooms of luminous delicacy.

Although it only flowers once in early summer, it is still a very valuable variety, having a wonderfully strong myrrh fragrance.

A vigorous climber, it can reach a height of 6m (20ft) and is ideal for softening structures or creating height in the garden. Try clothing a wall, a trellis or a pergola with this beautiful rose for stunning effect. It isn't too demanding, doing well in full or partial sunlight, facing in any direction and in all soil types.

If your aim is to train your climbing rose up a wall, make sure you dig your hole directly against the wall, adding a generous forkful of farmyard manure as you dig. You will be rewarded with fragrant blooms at the perfect height for appreciating their beauty.

David Austin Roses, Bowling Green Lane, Albrighton, Wolverhampton, WV7 2HB. Tel: 01902 376 328.
Email: help@davidaustinroses.co.uk. www.davidaustinroses.co.uk.
See also: The Rose Society UK. www.therosesociety.org.uk.

Constance Spry

Constance Spry might well have been described as a 'lifestyle guru' except that, in her lifetime, the term hadn't been invented and though she made her name in advising other women on how to create beautiful homes and wonderful food, she came to her fame from very modest beginnings.

Constance Fletcher was born in Derby, the eldest child of a railway clerk who, thanks to his diligent extra-mural university studies, was offered a senior appointment in the Department of Agriculture in Ireland. The family moved there in 1901 and Constance began her studies at Alexandra College in Dublin. Initially, her interests were in nursing, hygiene and food analysis, enabling her by 1908 to take up a full-time appointment as a lecturer for the Women's National Health Association.

When Constance married in 1910, she found herself not only running a household but creating a garden and this was where she began to develop an interest in growing flowers for cutting. With the advent of WWI she made good use of her nursing knowledge by working with the Dublin Red Cross. But she was becoming extremely unhappy in her marriage, finally abandoning it in 1916 and moving back to England to work as a welfare officer, first at an engineering factory at Barrow-in-Furness, then at the Ministry of Munitions. Her personal life took a turn for the better, too, and she married her second husband, Henry Ernest Spry, in 1920. Her interest in flowers continued to grow and when she was appointed principal of a school which taught practical domestic skills to factory workers in south London, she added flower-arranging classes to lessons in cookery and dressmaking.

Her great interest was in 'old' roses and she began to take on commissions for floral decorations to grace the tables at her friends' dinner parties and weddings. The colours of these floral arrangements were inspired by Constance's love of sixteenth and seventeenth century Dutch flower paintings and by her own cherished collection of flower books. She also took a great delight in finding unusual and original containers for her arrangements, breaking away from the stiff, formal styles which had been popular up until then, often combining unusual and commonplace flowers with foliage, vegetables and fruit. Interest in her work was growing to such an extent that she was able to resign from her job at the school and turn her absorbing hobby into a business, opening her first shop in 1929. Her reputation was secured with a sensational, exquisite arrangement of hedgerow flowers in the window of an Old Bond Street perfumery.

Constance Spry's flower arranging was an art which was much appreciated by her clients, who now included members of the royal family. But in 1939, WWII forced a change of direction again and Constance went back to teaching. Whereas she had already written three books on flowers and gardens, she now began writing the first of her cookery books, encouraging the women of wartime Britain to grow and cook their own food. When the war ended, she and a friend, the eminent cook Rosemary Hume, set up the Cordon Bleu Cookery School and the two published what was to become a domestic 'classic' – *The Constance Spry Cookery Book*. It is still widely available.

Constance could never ignore the siren song of flowers and in 1947 she was asked to design the floral decorations to grace Westminster Abbey for the wedding of the Princess Elizabeth. Then, when the princess ascended the throne in 1952, Constance Spry again supervised the flowers, both in the Abbey and along the route of the royal procession. Her colleague Rosemary Hume, who was also involved in the preparations for the coronation, devised a dish for foreign dignitaries visiting London for the occasion and 'Coronation Chicken' remains popular to this day. Constance Spry was awarded an OBE in the coronation honours list and her name is immortalised – appropriately – in a vigorous, climbing 'old rose', the original English rose from the David Austin nursery.

BUSH ROSE
'ELIZABETH CASSON'

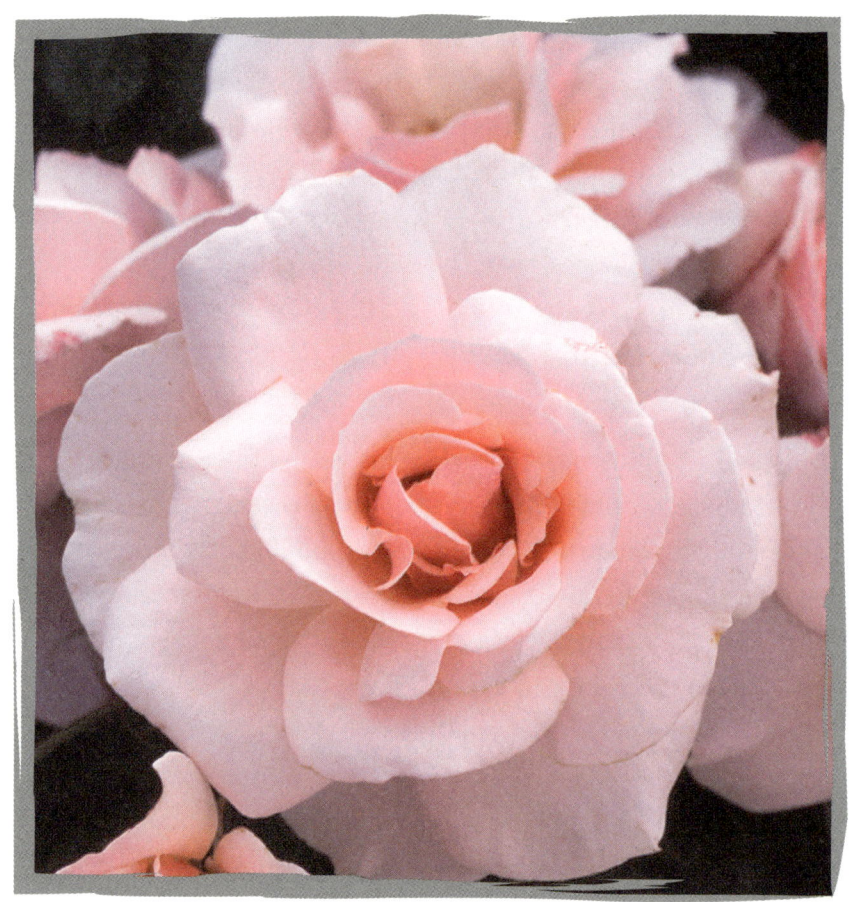

© Harkness Roses

Elizabeth Casson

1881-1954

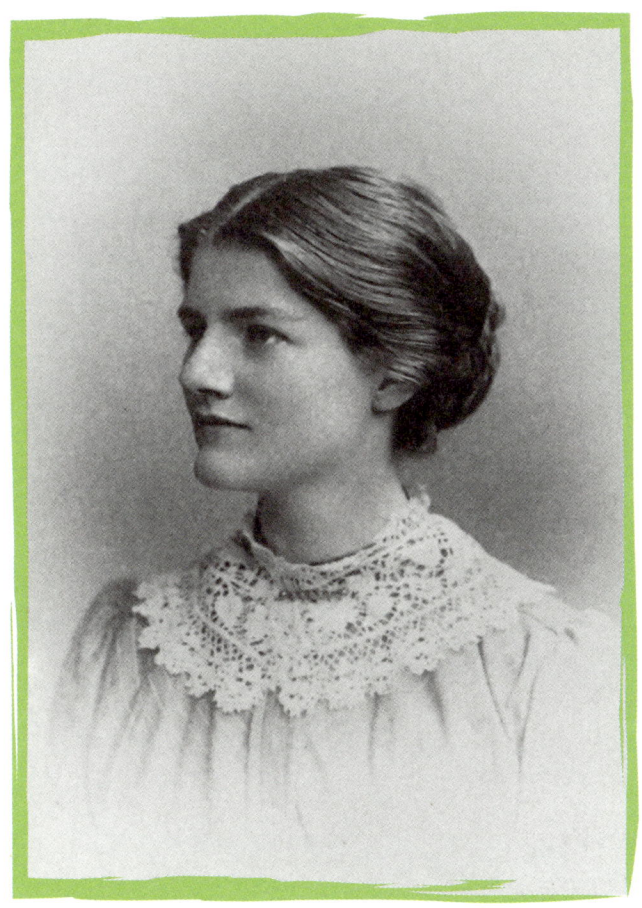

Elizabeth Casson at the age of twenty-one.

BUSH ROSE
'ELIZABETH CASSON'
IN YOUR GARDEN

Whether you grow this delightful rose in beds, borders, groups or hedges, it is one of the most rewarding of flowers because it looks attractive from spring right through until late autumn. Growing to approximately 90cm tall x 70cm wide (3ft x 2ft), it can be relied upon to give at least two flushes of flowers in the growing season.

The petals are long and elegant when at the bud stage and when the mature flowers develop, they are particularly pretty, with puffs of candy-floss pink revealing a graceful and charming flower form. With its dense, healthy foliage, bushy growth habit and the strong, fruity perfume of the flowers, this is a rose which is sure to impress.

Roses can get to look overgrown, raggedy and unloved unless they are pruned carefully during spring, when growth re-starts for the new season – it's always worth checking how best to do this for different types of roses. There is a wealth of advice online and, if you follow it carefully, your roses will reward you with magnificent flowers throughout the summer, often until the first frosts.

Harkness Roses, Cambridge Road, Hitchin, Herts, SG4 0JT.
Tel: 01462 420402. Email: harkness@roses.co.uk. www.roses.co.uk.
See also: The British Association of Rose Breeders. www.rosesuk.com.

Elizabeth Casson

The 'Elizabeth Casson' rose was launched at the Chelsea Flower Show in 2005, to mark the 50th anniversary of the death of the remarkable woman who first realised the importance of occupational therapy in the healing process.

Born in Denbigh, North Wales, on 14th April 1881, Elizabeth Casson was the third daughter of a local bank manager who was also an enthusiastic amateur organ builder. All seven children in the family were musical and artistic with strong socialist principles and when their father decided to turn his organ-building hobby into a living, he moved the whole family to London. Initially, the young Elizabeth took a secretarial course with the aim of helping her father in his organ-building business but, after his retirement, she searched elsewhere for work and the job she found marked a turning point in her life. In 1908, she took a post as a Housing Manager, working at the Red Cross Hall in Southwark for the social reformer Octavia Hill, and she remained there for five years. Casson's particular interest was in organising recreational activities for the residents of the Hall and she was keen to kindle their interest in craft work along with other arts-based activities. In this she was greatly encouraged by Octavia Hill herself and, in later years, Elizabeth Casson always said that her work in occupational therapy owed a great deal to her employer's influence.

Then, at the age of thirty in October 1913, despite a struggle to acquire sufficient Latin to pass the entrance examination, Elizabeth Casson entered the University of Bristol to study medicine, becoming the first female doctor of medicine ever to emerge from that university and going on to pursue what was destined to be a very distinguished career. Having graduated, she went on to develop a specialist interest in the care of patients with mental ill health and in 1927 she was awarded the coveted Gaskell Prize and Medal of the Royal Medico-Psychological Association.

One Christmas, during the course of her psychiatric hospital experience, Dr Casson noticed the rapt attention with which some of her women patients were concentrating on making some simple Christmas decorations. Thinking about what she'd seen, she began to realise the therapeutic benefits and real sense of achievement which creative tasks and activities like this could bring to a patient's convalescence. To explore this idea further, she went the United States, where she visited the occupational therapy department of a New York hospital and also the School of Occupational Therapy at Boston's Tufts University. What she saw there convinced her that she was right. So in 1929, on her return from the US, she sent her older brother, the eminent actor Sir Lewis Casson, a brief telegram containing one question.

It said simply, '*Can you lend me a thousand pounds?*' The even greater brevity of the reply delighted her. '*Yes.*'

It was all Elizabeth needed. With the money, she set about the purchase of Dorset House in The Promenade at Clifton in Bristol, where she was able to realise her dream of establishing her own residential clinic for 'women with mental disorders'. Here, in 1930, she founded the UK's first School of Occupational Therapy and became its Medical Director. It took hard work and selfless dedication but it is thanks to Dr. Elizabeth Casson's pioneering vision that Occupational Therapy is now fully recognized in the UK as an important health care discipline.

The Elizabeth Casson Trust was established in 1948 and perpetuates her name in all aspects of education and training within the discipline. The Trust also enabled a close relationship between the occupational therapists of Dorset House and their counterparts at Tufts University in Boston, with an exchange of scholarship students between the two. In 1951 Dr Casson was awarded the OBE in recognition of her achievements and was elected an Honorary Fellow of the World Federation of Occupational Therapists. The Dr Elizabeth Casson annual memorial lecture was established in 1973 and each lecturer is now honoured with the gift of an Elizabeth Casson rose.

PRIMULA MARGINATA
'ELIZABETH FRY'

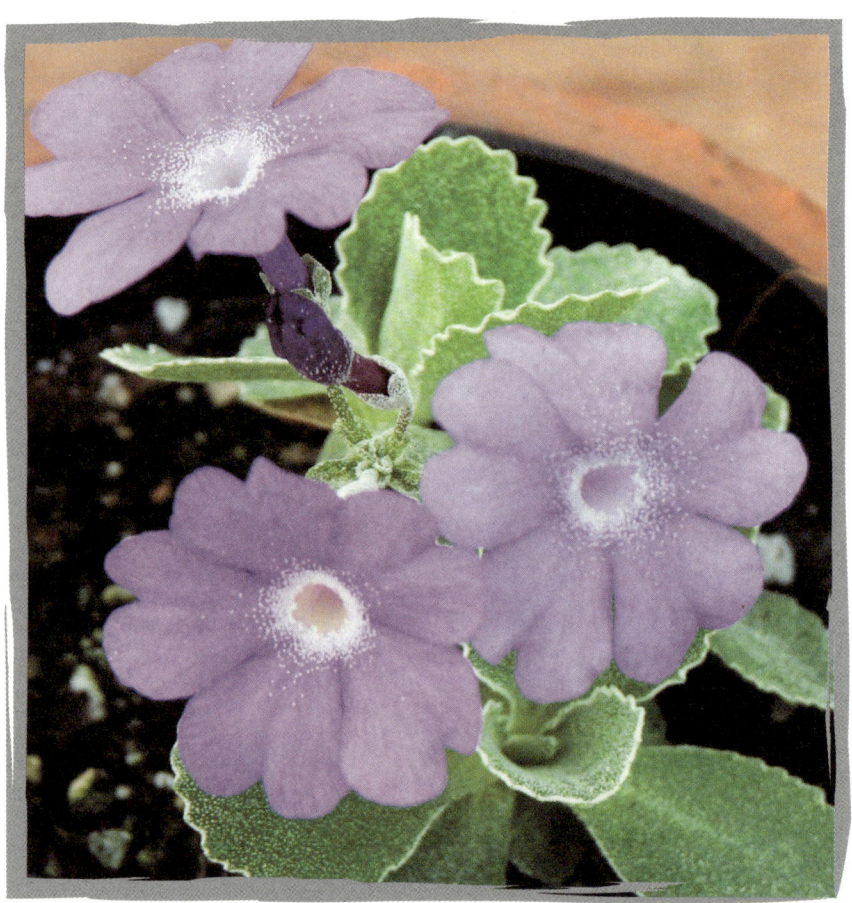

© Jodie Mitchell at Barnhaven Primroses

Elizabeth Fry

1780-1845

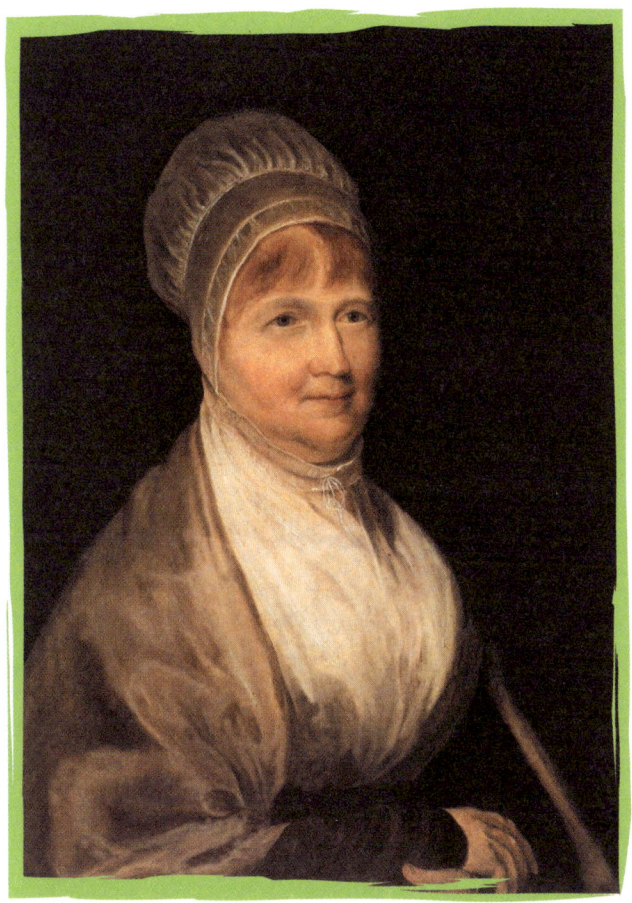

Such is the high regard for Elizabeth Fry that she was the first woman, other than the Queen, to be depicted on a British bank note.

PRIMULA MARGINATA
'ELIZABETH FRY'
IN YOUR GARDEN

Just like its inspirational namesake, *Primula marginata* 'Elizabeth Fry' rewards the gardener with hope and anticipation even in the darkest days of mid-winter because this is when it makes its first appearance.

This wonderful little survivor is hardy down to -30°C (-22°F) and the emergence of its flowers is one of the earliest signs that spring has begun to make its welcome return.

The flowers themselves are small and pale lilac in colour with a darker eye, a welcome sight as they begin to appear among the attractive, toothed evergreen leaves.

This good-natured plant is perfectly contented to grow in partial shade and, indeed, in any type of soil, acid, alkaline or neutral, provided that it is well-drained. Eventually reaching a height of 5cm-10cm (2in-4in), it is equally contented in a pot, a trough or a rockery.

Barnhaven Primroses, Keranguiner, 22310, Plestin-les-grèves, France.
Tel: +33 (0)296 356 841. Email: info@barnhaven.com. www.barnhaven.com.
See also: The National Auricula & Primula Society UK.
www.auriculaandprimula.org.uk.

Elizabeth Fry

If the names Cadbury, Rowntree and Fry make your mouth water, it's because these families have all been famous manufacturers of chocolates in Britain since the early nineteenth century. And the reason is simple: because they were all Quakers and committed to the temperance movement, they began to produce cocoa drinks as a cost effective and healthy alternative to alcohol, which they saw as the major cause of deprivation in the poorer classes. Social reform was one of their core principles.

Elizabeth Gurney was already a Quaker when she married into the Fry family in 1800. She too had come from what was a strong Quaker background in Norwich, where she had heard a sermon by the itinerant Quaker preacher William Savery. Inspired by his message, Elizabeth's religious beliefs now became central to her life and she adopted Quaker dress and speech. Her parents both came from banking families, her father a partner in Gurney's Bank and her mother's family had been among the founders of Barclay's Bank. They approved of their daughter's marriage to Joseph Fry, the son of an orthodox and wealthy Quaker family.

Now living in London, Joseph and Elizabeth Fry settled into married life and in 1808 Joseph, too, became a banker. Elizabeth was busy raising eleven children but despite her domestic responsibilities she managed to do a considerable amount of work in the community. She distributed clothing, food and medicine and was acknowledged as a Quaker minister, relying on her husband's support in her charitable activities.

The first time Elizabeth Fry visited Newgate prison in 1813, she was appalled by what she found there. Several hundred female prisoners, along with their children, were packed into filthy, overcrowded cells where they slept on straw. Here they did their cooking and washing as best they could. Hardened criminals were locked up alongside first offenders and some had not even had a fair trial. Elizabeth was determined that she would help them and prison reform became a motivating force in her life. Knowing the importance of education, she established a small school for the prisoners' children, determined to teach them to expect something good out of life. She persuaded the authorities to establish a system of classification and, in order to improve the prisoners' health, she urged the appointment of a prison matron. Many of these prisoners were punished for their crimes by being sent to a penal colony in Australia. They were routinely taken to the docks with their children in open carts, only to be humiliated by crowds of people who jeered and pelted them with rotten fruit. Elizabeth campaigned for them to have the privacy of covered carriages for this journey. She also issued them with special packages containing useful items like cutlery, sewing kits with scraps of fabric and, always, a bible. At the docks, she talked the captains of the convict ships bound for

Australia into improving the conditions on board. Thus began her work to help start the movement towards the abolition of transportation to the colonies. This became law in 1837.

Little by little, word spread about the remarkable humanitarian work she was doing and the successes she had achieved. Queen Victoria held Elizabeth Fry's dedication in high regard, granting her frequent audiences and contributing money to her cause. Fry wrote and spoke widely on the need for prison reform, inspiring others to follow her example and, in 1840, she opened a training school for nurses. This was much admired by Florence Nightingale who took a team of trained nurses from the school to assist her in her work among wounded soldiers in the Crimean War.

Elizabeth Fry died in 1845 and the London Borough of Hackney, anxious to pay tribute to her, established a refuge in her name. It was the first of very many memorials to this compassionate, determined and committed campaigner for social reform.

SEA HOLLY
'MISS WILLMOTT'S GHOST'

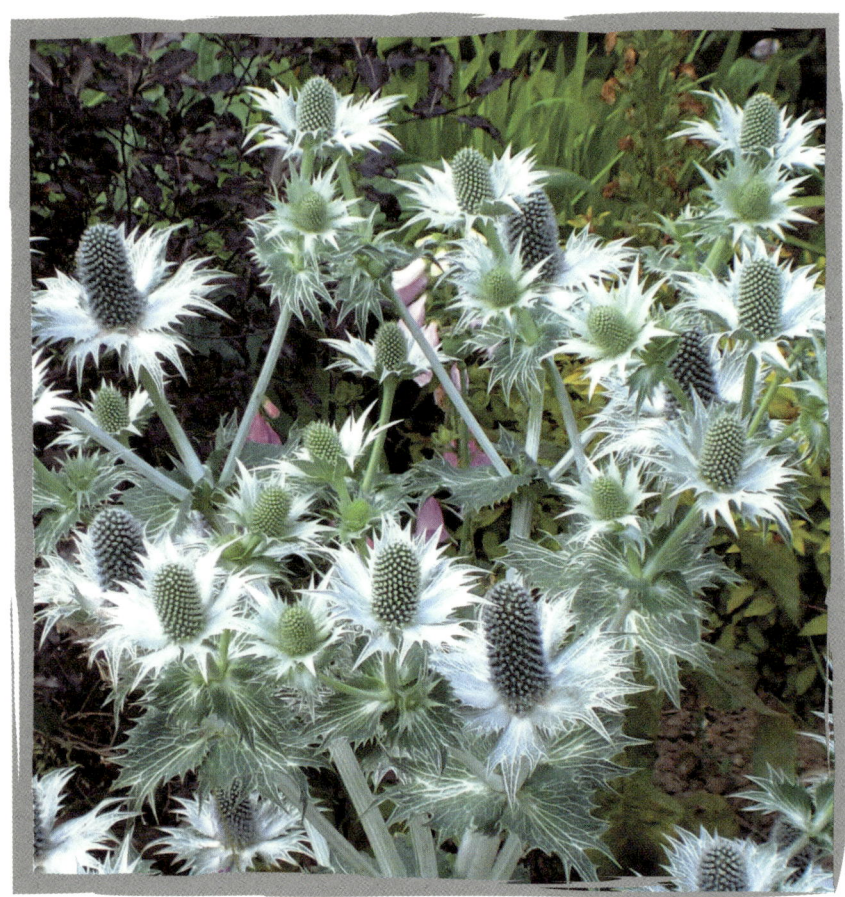

© Dorset Perennials

Ellen Willmott

1858-1934

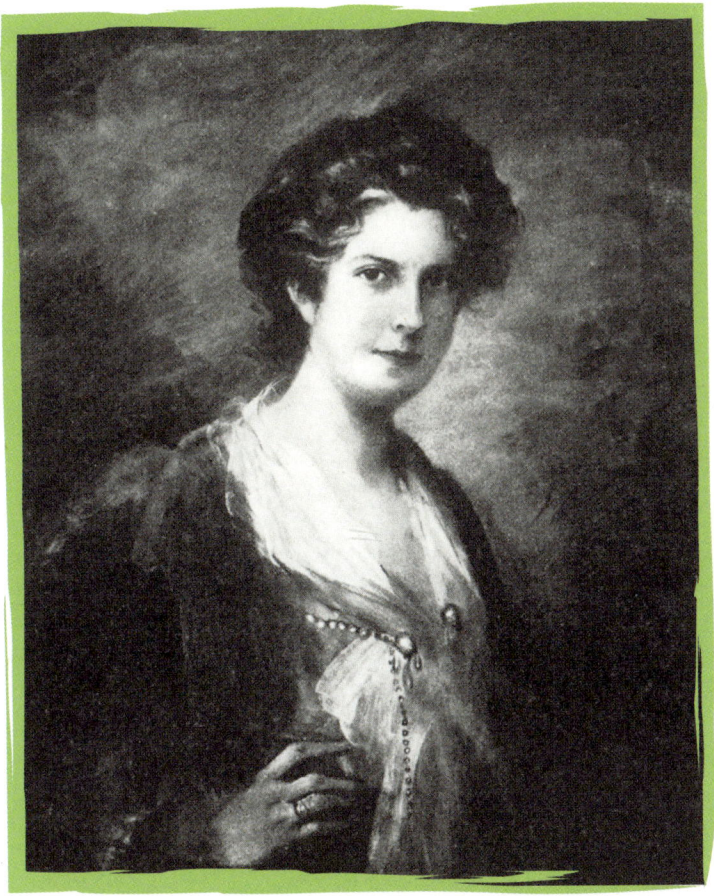

Not just one but nearly sixty plants have been named for this eminent horticulturalist.

SEA HOLLY
'MISS WILLMOTT'S GHOST'
IN YOUR GARDEN

Eryngium giganteum, to give it its proper name, is a surprisingly attractive addition to the herbaceous border, growing up to 1 metre (3ft) high. Marvellously architectural-looking, it acquired its name from Ellen Willmott's habit of carrying seeds of it in her pocket and sprinkling them in the gardens she visited, silently leaving a 'ghostly' trail in her wake! And, with its silver white cones, surrounded by large silver bracts, it is an eerie presence in the half-light.

Close inspection of the flower heads shows that each is in fact a composite head of many smaller flowers and these are much prized by flower arrangers for their excellent drying qualities.

As a rule, sea hollies prefer a well-drained root run in full sun and will tolerate excessive lime, gravel and poor soils. In colder, wetter areas, it is wise to remove dead foliage from the crown before the onset of winter, to avoid crown rot.

It is a very hardy herbaceous perennial and can withstand temperatures as low as -20°C (-4°F). Depending on its situation, the plant can behave as a biennial or short-lived perennial but, either way, it will obligingly self-seed to provide replacements.

Dorset Perennials, Holnest Sherbourne, Dorset, DT9 5PR. Tel: 01963 210643. Email: sales@dorsetperennials.co.uk. www.dorsetperennials.co.uk. See also: RHS advice. www.rhs.org.uk/Plants.

Ellen Willmott

It is no exaggeration to say that little Ellie Willmott enjoyed a hugely privileged childhood, brought up as she was in a home where money flowed like water. Legend has it that, on the morning of her seventh birthday, the envelope beside her plate at breakfast contained not only a birthday greeting but a cheque for £1,000. As 'birthday money' goes, that was a very generous gift in 1865! And gifts continued to be showered upon her and her younger sisters by generous relatives, by her mother, who was independently wealthy, and her father, who had made his fortune 'in the city'.

Following the death of Ellie's youngest sister, Ada, the family moved to Warley Place in Essex, where the remaining two cherished daughters, Ellie and Rose, were encouraged to follow the traditions established in their mother's family, of taking an active interest in the gardens and orchards of their home. Once kindled, Ellie's enthusiasm for gardening never waned, becoming an overwhelming passion as she grew up. On her twenty-first birthday, her father wrote proudly of the alpines she was planting in the new rockery. He bought another twenty acres of land and all four members of the family were involved in the planning and planting of what had become an extensive estate. To celebrate Ellie's thirtieth birthday, the family undertook a grand tour of Europe and Ellie, now a wealthy young woman in her own right, set about the purchase of a French chateau. Thereafter, she divided her time between Le Chateau de Tresserve in Aix-les-Bains and her home in Warley Place, avidly buying huge numbers of plants for both gardens.

Ellie never married though her sister Rose did and moved away from home when Ellie was in her early thirties. When her parents died, Ellen (as she now preferred to be known) inherited everything. With generous legacies from her godmother and both parents, she was now a fabulously rich woman and her gardens became her total obsession. She employed one hundred gardeners and woe betide any gardener who allowed a weed to thrive: that meant instant dismissal! At around this time, she also acquired another property abroad and funded several plant-hunting expeditions to China and to the Middle East. Some sixty of the specimens brought back from these expeditions were named in her honour, examples include *Ceratostigma willmottianum*, *Rosa willmottiae* and *Corylopsis willmottiae*.

An enthusiastic and prominent member of the Royal Horticultural Society, Ellen Willmott served on several of its specialist plant committees and when the RHS established its Victoria Medal of Honour in 1897 to celebrate Queen Victoria's Diamond Jubilee, she was one of the only two women to be awarded the distinction: the other was Gertrude Jekyll. Appointed a Trustee of the RHS Gardens at Wisley in 1903, two years later Ellen became one of the first women to be elected a fellow of the Linnean Society of London, the world's oldest active biological society. She was an effective writer, too – there were two books by Ellen Willmott, one about her own garden at Warley Place along with *The Genus Rosa*, a definitive guide to roses which was published in two parts.

Her lavish lifestyle and profligate spending habits meant that she eventually faced financial difficulties. Forced to sell her properties abroad to pay her bills, she began to hoard her possessions, installing booby traps on her estate to deter potential thieves, and she developed the distressing habit of carrying a revolver in her handbag! Towards the end of her life, this autocratic woman, always so beautifully dressed and with a large personal staff in attendance, was forced to live in relative poverty with only one faithful butler left to attend her. She died alone in 1934 and after her death, her beloved Warley Place was sold off to pay her debts. Though the house was eventually demolished, the grounds became a nature reserve in the green belt of Essex.

ENGLISH SHRUB ROSE
'LADY EMMA HAMILTON'

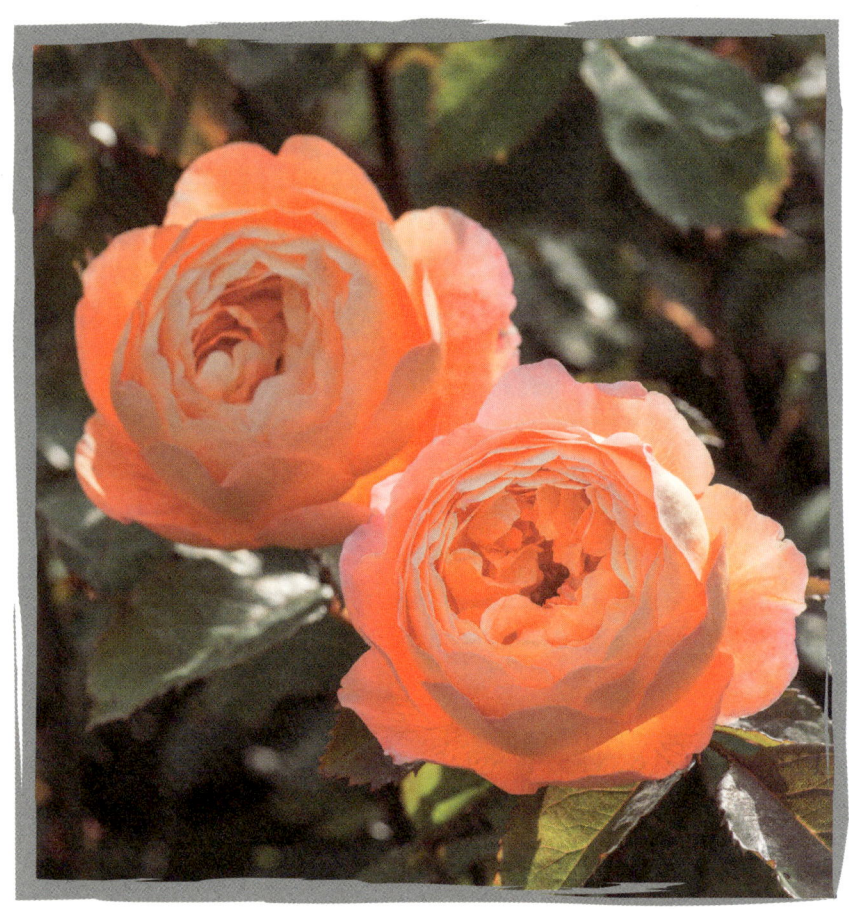

© David Austin Roses

Emma Hamilton

1765–1815

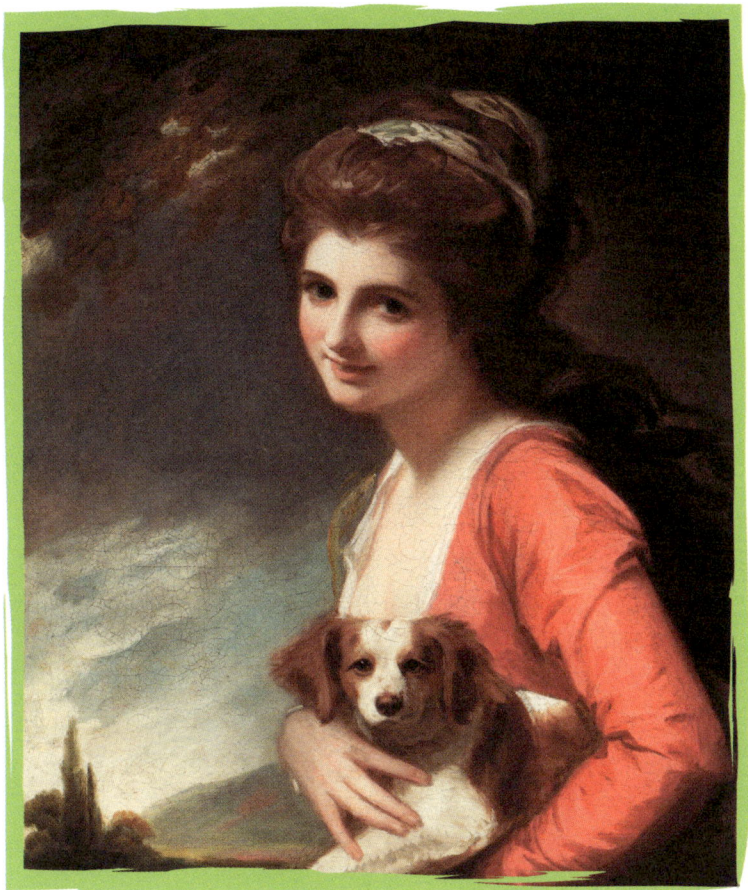

Emma Hamilton in one of her many portraits by George Romney.

ENGLISH SHRUB ROSE 'LADY EMMA HAMILTON'
IN YOUR GARDEN

An English shrub rose which is as warmly beautiful as its namesake. Dark red buds with dashes of orange open to chalice-shaped blooms of rich tangerine-orange, with yellow-orange on the outside of the petals. These are held dramatically against very dark, polished, bronzy-green leaves that slowly become a darker green with age.

The flowers have a strong, delicious, fruity fragrance with hints of pear, grape and citrus fruits. The growth is fairly upright but quite broad and bushy. It will reach a height and spread of 90cm x 90cm (3ft x 3ft) and is ideal for pots and containers but is equally happy in a rose border or a mixed border.

If you avoid a north-facing aspect, you will find that Lady Emma Hamilton thrives in all soil types and does best in full sunlight, flowering repeatedly throughout the growing season. It will also grace any display of cut flowers.

David Austin Roses, Bowling Green Lane, Albrighton, Wolverhampton, WV7 2HB. Tel: 01902 376 328. Email: help@davidaustinroses.co.uk. www.davidaustinroses.co.uk.
See also: The Rose Society UK. www.therosesociety.org.uk.

Emma Hamilton

In celebration of the 200th anniversary of the Battle of Trafalgar, won so gloriously in 1805 by the English fleet under Vice-Admiral Horatio Lord Nelson (1758-1805), the David Austin nursery named a new rose after the great man's mistress, Lady Emma Hamilton.

Emma Hamilton was instinctively a survivor, a real chameleon, changing her name and her loyalties whenever life threw another problem her way. Born in poverty into the family of an illiterate blacksmith in Cheshire, she was christened Amy Lyon. Her father died when she was two months old and little Amy was brought up by her mother in Hawarden, Flintshire. Sometime later when the two had moved to London, young Amy began to work as a housemaid for a Dr. Thomas Linley, a theatre impresario and he might well have been the one who suggested that she could find work as an actress. After all, she was an arrestingly pretty, vivacious girl with wide eyes and a classically straight nose. What is certain is that she developed a taste for the theatrical life, changed her name to Emma Lyon and was soon working as a dancer and a model.

It wasn't long before the lovely Miss Lyon caught the attention of a patron, a young man-about-town by the name of Sir Harry Fetherstonhaugh, who occasionally required her to dance naked on a table for the entertainment of his friends at stag parties.

Little wonder that Emma became pregnant and therefore superfluous but she was befriended by the Hon. Charles Francis Greville, with whom she fell in love. Soon Emma became his mistress and it wasn't long before she moved into his house in Paddington. Wanting a portrait of her, Greville commissioned one from the artist George Romney and Romney soon became obsessed with Emma's beauty, painting her sometimes as a nude or dressed up as any one of several famous characters from history. She appeared on canvas after canvas as Medea, Circe, Cassandra or just as Emma Hart – having changed her name yet again.

Greville seemed as genuinely fond of her as she was of him but he was also genuinely short of money and needed to marry an heiress rather than marry Emma. So she became the innocent victim of a plot. Suggesting a holiday, Greville sent Emma and her mother to Italy where his uncle, the diplomat Sir William Hamilton, a childless widower, was British Ambassador to the Court of Naples and in need of a hostess at the embassy. Emma was perfect for the role but when she realised that she was not expected to return to England she was absolutely furious at having been tricked by Greville. In a fit of pique, she married the 60-year-old Sir William, thus becoming Lady Hamilton. During this period, she took her 'dressing up' for Romney's paintings a stage further, developing a series of what she called her 'Attitudes', entertaining Embassy guests by inviting them to guess which character from history she was portraying. Among those guests who applauded her delightedly was Lord Nelson, the great hero of the British nation after his celebrated naval victories during the Napoleonic wars. Sir William greatly admired Nelson and always more than happy to welcome him as a guest in his home or to visit him on board his flagship in Naples harbour. Emma admired Nelson too; in fact, she couldn't resist him, even though by now he had lost an arm, the sight of one eye and several teeth. Sir William encouraged the relationship. Nelson's own marriage had been foundering for several years and in November 1800 he finally left his wife, moving into a rented house with Sir William and Lady Hamilton. From then on the three of them maintained a ménage á trois until Sir William's death in 1803. Emma and Nelson continued to live together at Merton Lodge in Wimbledon, but, despite Emma's wish that he would settle down and enter Parliament, Nelson returned to active service and two years later was killed at the Battle of Trafalgar. Emma, who had always been rather a spendthrift, was left with very little but a small pension from Sir William which didn't last long. To escape her many creditors, she finally fled to France with her daughter Horatia, her only surviving child by Nelson. She died, penniless, in Calais in 1815.

ENGLISH SHRUB ROSE
'EMILY BRONTË'

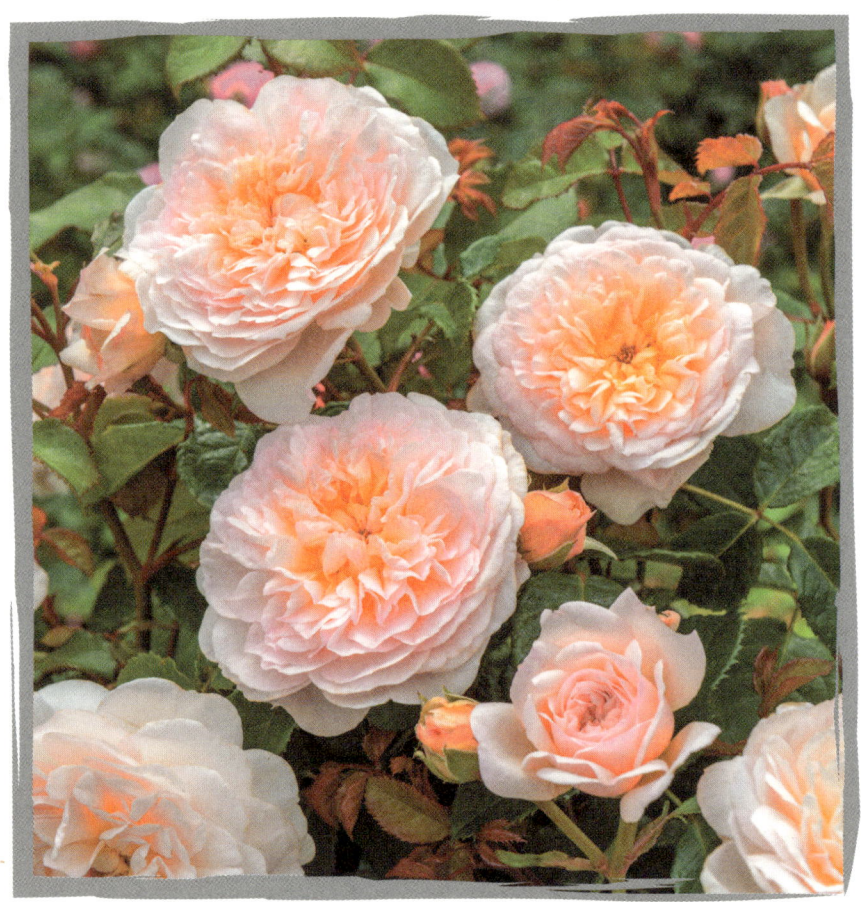

© David Austin Roses

Emily Brontë

1818-1848

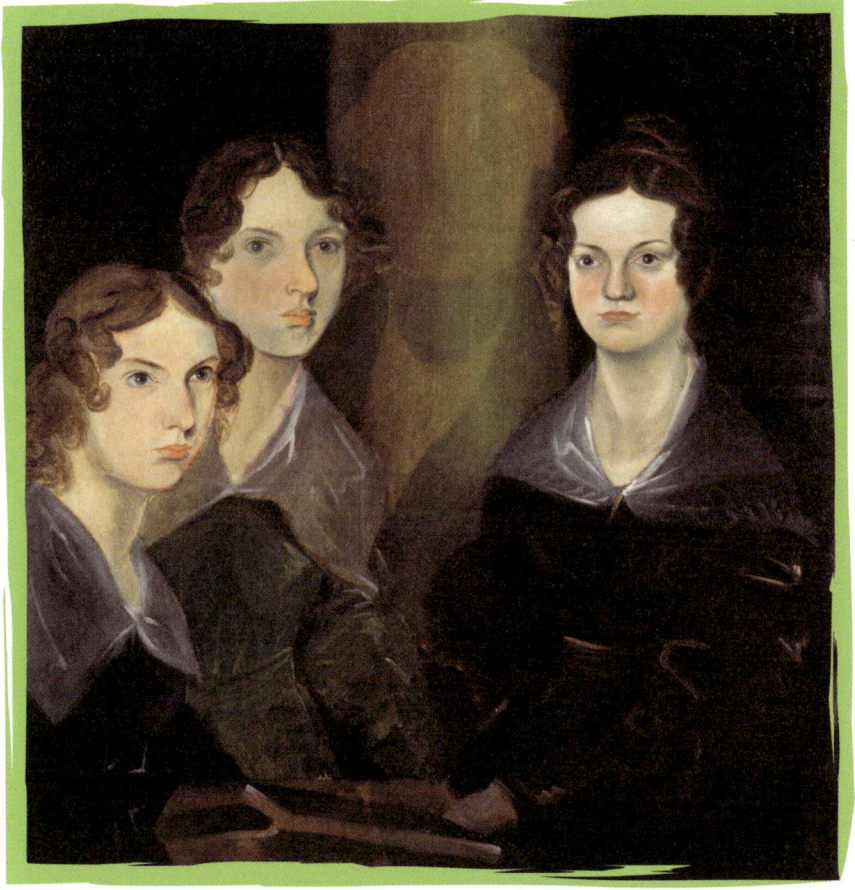

From left to right, Anne, Emily and Charlotte painted by their brother, Branwell, who had originally included himself in the picture. He later changed his mind and painted himself out of it, leaving only a ghostly image at the centre of the group.

ENGLISH SHRUB ROSE 'EMILY BRONTË'

IN YOUR GARDEN

At the request of the Brontë Society, this rose was named to celebrate the bicentenary of the birth of Emily Brontë.

It is an exceptionally beautiful rose with distinctive, strongly fragrant blooms that are very neat and rather flat. Each bloom is a lovely soft pink, with a subtle apricot hue, the smaller central petals deepening to rich apricot and surrounding a button eye, which unfurls to reveal deep-set stamens.

It flowers repeatedly throughout the growing season and, as the flowers develop, their strong tea fragrance becomes more 'old rose', with delicious hints of lemon and grapefruit.

With a spread of around 137cm x 137cm (4.5ft x 4.5ft), it will – like most shrub roses – perform surprisingly well in partial shade and is ideal in a mixed border or in a large patio pot.

A bushy shrub with strong, healthy, upright growth, it thrives in most soil types and in any position except north-facing.

David Austin Roses, Bowling Green Lane, Albrighton, Wolverhampton, WV7 2HB. Tel: 01902 376 328. Email: help@davidaustinroses.co.uk. www.davidaustinroses.co.uk. See also: The British Association of Rose Breeders. www.rosesuk.com.

Emily Brontë

No one can be sure exactly why young Patrick Brunty of County Down in Northern Ireland changed his name. But when this clever young man won a scholarship to university in 1802, the move to Cambridge was a seismic shift for the son of a poor Irish tenant farmer. So perhaps he felt that if he had a more aristocratic-sounding surname, he could fit in better with his privileged fellow-students at St. John's College. Unwittingly, he created a name which was destined to echo within the hallowed sanctum of the world's great literature. Because three of the Rev. Patrick Brontë's five daughters were the celebrated English authors Charlotte, Emily and Anne.

The family is strongly associated with Haworth, a hilltop village in the heart of West Yorkshire, now universally known as 'Brontë Country'. They had previously lived in Thornton, some twelve miles away, near Bradford, where money had been scarce, but things became easier with the move to Haworth in 1820. The Rev. Brontë's appointment to the living gave him security of tenure and a large parsonage in which he, his wife and six children could live rent-free. However, this happy state of affairs did not last long because his much-loved wife died within eighteen months, so her sister, Elizabeth Branwell, who had nursed her through her terminal illness, stayed on to look after the family.

In the circumstances, it seemed expedient to send the older girls to a residential school for daughters of the clergy but that had disastrous consequences. The two older sisters, Maria and Elizabeth, both succumbed to a typhoid epidemic while they were at the school and were sent home, only to die almost immediately. Thereafter the three remaining sisters and their brother Branwell, were kept at home to be educated by their father and aunt. This was an informal, unstructured way of learning and the girls, unusually for those days, had access to a wide range of published material, books and magazines, which they read voraciously. In the enclosed atmosphere of the parsonage, the three girls began to make up stories to amuse themselves and when Branwell was given a box of toy soldiers for his birthday, his sisters created a complete fantasy world for them. Then, when Emily was just thirteen, she and her sister Anne began to write about the myths and legends of an imaginary island called Gondal. Poetry followed, too, filling the pages of notebooks until in time, their older sister Charlotte, also a poet, suggested they should try to publish their work. Reluctantly, Anne and Emily agreed and, using money from a legacy left by their aunt who had since died, they set about self-publishing their work. As young women, they thought they might achieve more credibility if they took male pseudonyms but they wanted to retain their initials. So the collection was published as *Poems by Currer, Ellis and Acton Bell*. There were some sixty poems in all but the collection sold only two copies. However, one critic singled out the poems by 'Ellis Bell' as having great potential.

This didn't change Emily's attitude to life. She had always been an intensely private person, only rarely taking anyone other than her sister Anne into her confidence. After her aunt's death, Emily had assumed responsibility for running the parsonage where her closest companions were her dog, 'Keeper', and a pet hawk, which seemed to symbolise her love of the rugged beauty of the Yorkshire moors. By now each of the three sisters had started to write novels and, again under the same pseudonym, the powerful, passionate novel *Wuthering Heights* by Ellis Bell was published in 1847.

At first, the critics, accustomed to the more genteel qualities of Victorian literature, were puzzled and frankly hostile because Emily's compelling story was about 'real' people, poor people who lived real lives. She herself didn't live to see what the book became because Branwell, her brother, suddenly died in September 1848 of tuberculosis, masked by his alcoholism. At his funeral, Emily caught a cold and, refusing treatment, she became so weak that she herself was dead within three months at the age of thirty. She never knew that her only novel would eventually be acknowledged a masterpiece, becoming one of the most consistently popular books in the English language.

NIGELLA DAMASCENA
'MISS JEKYLL'

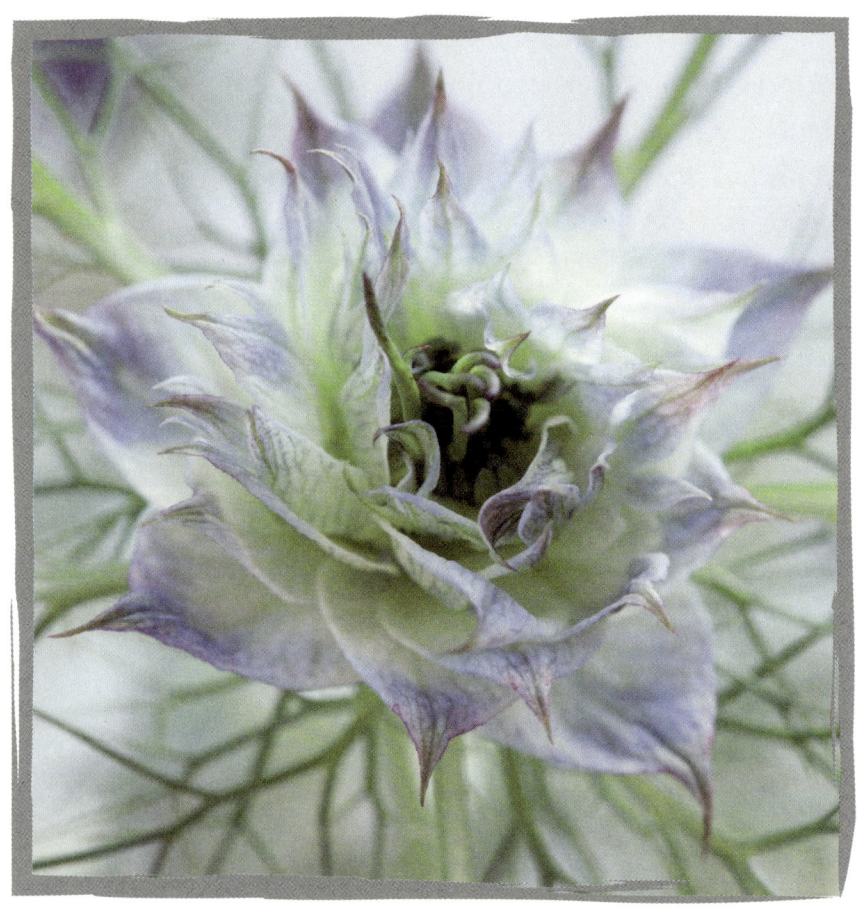

Nigella Damascena 'Miss Jekyll' © Chiltern Seeds

Pretty Maids

Gertrude Jekyll

1843–1932

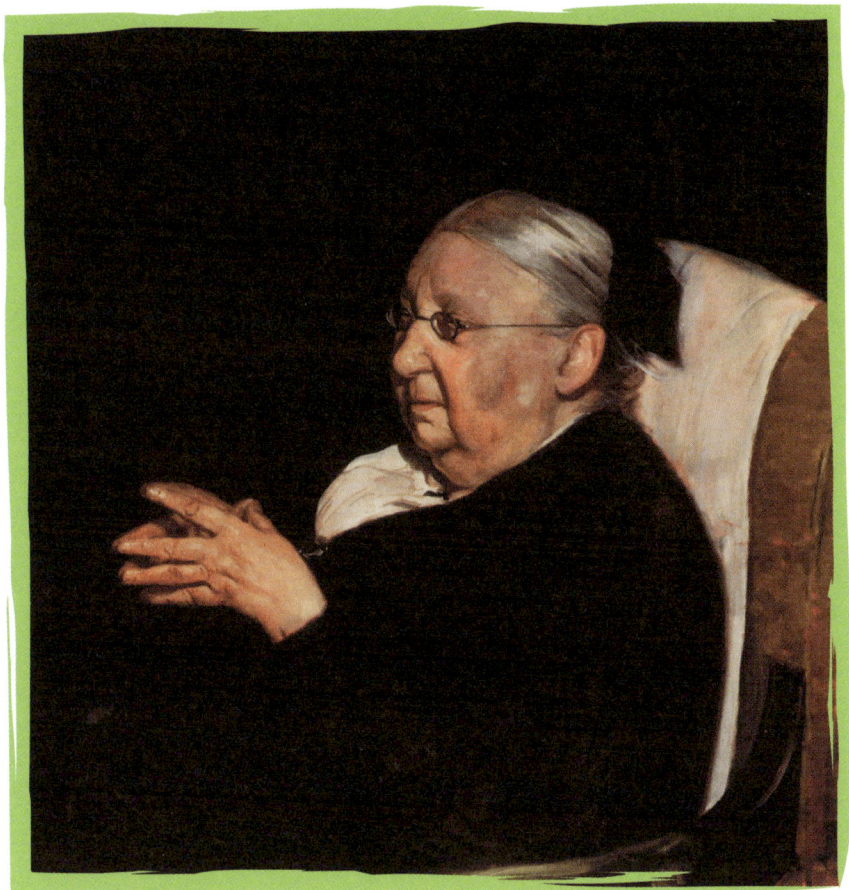

Gertrude loathed having to sit for her portrait and could be quite difficult about it. In 1920, she kept the artist William Nicholson waiting so long for this sitting that he amused himself by painting a picture of her gardening boots!

NIGELLA DAMASCENA
'MISS JEKYLL'
IN YOUR GARDEN

A long-established favourite in the garden and in cultivation for many, many years, this is a particularly beautiful variety of *Nigella damascena*.

Fully hardy throughout the British Isles, it is also known by its more fanciful name of 'Love-in-a-Mist', a name suggested perhaps by bright, light-blue flowers against typically ferny foliage.

Agreeably easy to grow, the seed can be sown in autumn for an early display the following year, or between March and May when all danger of frost has passed. The fine seeds should be sown directly into a prepared, weed-free seed-bed at a depth of 3mm (1/8in) in rows 30cm (11in) apart.

Germination after a spring sowing occurs within ten to twenty-one days and when the seedlings are large enough to handle, they should be thinned to approx. 25cm (9in) apart. This will reward the gardener with a beautiful display of large, semi-double flowers which are most attractive to pollinating insects.

Chiltern Seeds Ltd, Crowmarsh Battle Barns, 114, Preston Crowmarsh, Wallingford, OX10 6SL. Tel: 01491 824675.
Email: info@chilternseeds.co.uk. www.chilternseeds.co.uk.
See also: RHS advice. www.rhs.org.uk/Plants.

Gertrude Jekyll

'The lesson I have thoroughly learnt, and wish to pass on to others,' wrote Gertrude Jekyll, 'is to know the enduring happiness that the love of a garden gives.' Miss Jekyll, as she was widely and respectfully known, was the doyenne of garden designers who brought her knowledge of art and her love of colour and symmetry to bear on everything she did.

Born into a very distinguished family with close links to the monarchy, Gertrude Jekyll was educated by governesses at home in Surrey and showed early promise as an artist, sketching many of her parents' influential friends. In 1861 she enrolled in the National School of Art in South Kensington and within a few years, her paintings were being exhibited by the Society of Female Artists and at the Royal Academy. But, truth to tell, there was little that this witty, clever young woman couldn't turn her hand to and everything she touched was approached with method, professionalism and consummate craftsmanship. She took the same approach to carving, gilding, wood inlaying, embroidery, modelling, quilting, house painting, a little art blacksmithing and, above all, gardening.

In 1863 and again in 1864, Gertrude Jekyll travelled around the Mediterranean with some friends and was profoundly affected by the landscapes, architecture and colours she saw in Turkey, Rhodes and Greece. Above all, she was enchanted by the plants and began busily collecting those which took her fancy. These Mediterranean trips had a great influence on her later work and she was guided by a simple, straightforward principle – her designs answered the question of what a garden was meant to be to the person for whom it was designed. For her, *'the first purpose of a garden is to be a place of quiet beauty such as will give delight to the eye and repose and refreshment to the mind'.*

When her father died in 1876, her mother commissioned the building of a home for herself and her daughter at Munstead Heath in Surrey. Gertrude laid out the garden to her own design and it became the precursor to the garden of her own home, Munstead Wood, built nearby in 1895. Once completed, the garden became a magnet for the gardeners and artists of the time who greatly admired all aspects of it. One visitor observed that the garden had 'deservedly attained a universal reputation for excellence'. By now Miss Jekyll was collecting clients as well as plants and during the following years, she designed gardens for hospitals, colleges, schools, churches and charities, as well as for the great and the good who so admired her work. She wrote fourteen books on garden design and contributed regular articles to the popular press. In 1897 she was one of the only two women to be awarded the Victoria Medal of Honour of the Royal Horticultural Society: the other was Ellen Willmott. Gertrude Jekyll was absolutely delighted when, in responding on her behalf at the medal ceremony, Samuel Hole, Dean of Rochester and himself a noted horticulturalist, referred to her as 'The Queen of Spades'. And that was an apt description because, by now, her garden at Munstead Wood adjoined a plant nursery, which she ran with the help of one other plantsman. Each year, thousands of plants were dispatched to clients all over the country and she continued to supply them for thirty-five years until her death in 1932.

As a garden designer, Gertrude Jekyll achieved her greatest successes in collaboration with several distinguished architects, foremost among them her friend Sir Edwin Lutyens. Their dynamic partnership can be appreciated in the restored Edwardian garden at Hestercombe in Somerset, which they worked on between 1904 and 1908. Here, Gertrude Jekyll's planting and sense of colour enhance the lines, levels, water features, hidden bowers and surprise views of the Lutyens hard landscaping, the whole created with natural materials and superb craftsmanship.

Miss Jekyll certainly proved that *the love of gardening is a seed once sown that never dies.*

CLIMBING ROSE
'GLORIANA'

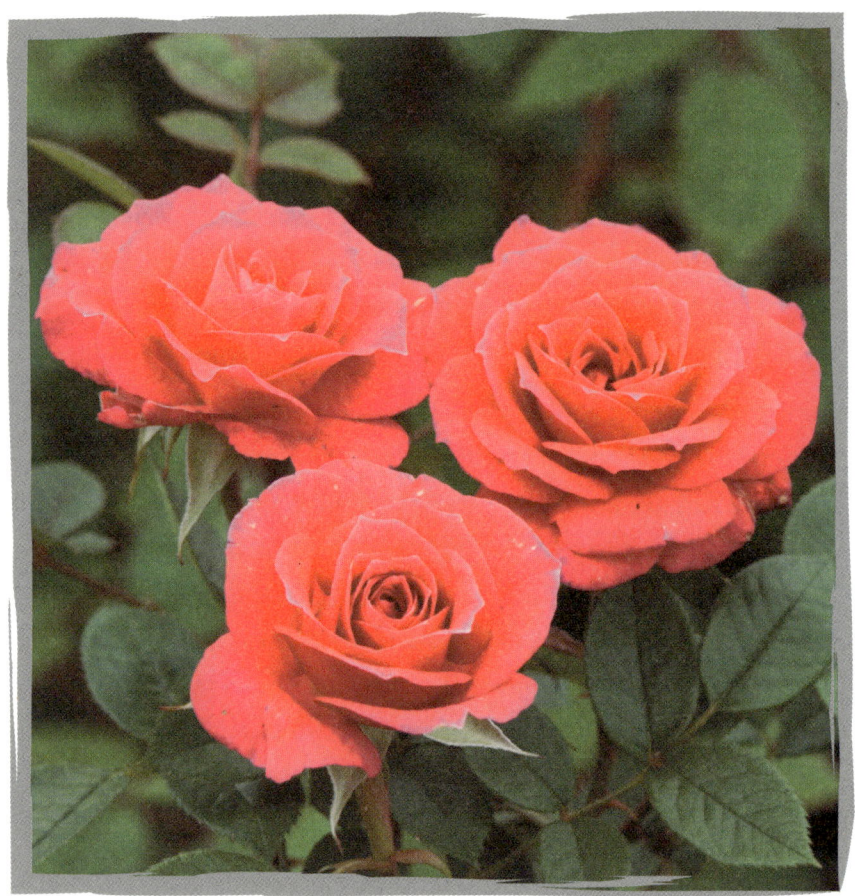

© David Austin Roses

Gloriana (Queen Elizabeth I)

1533-1603

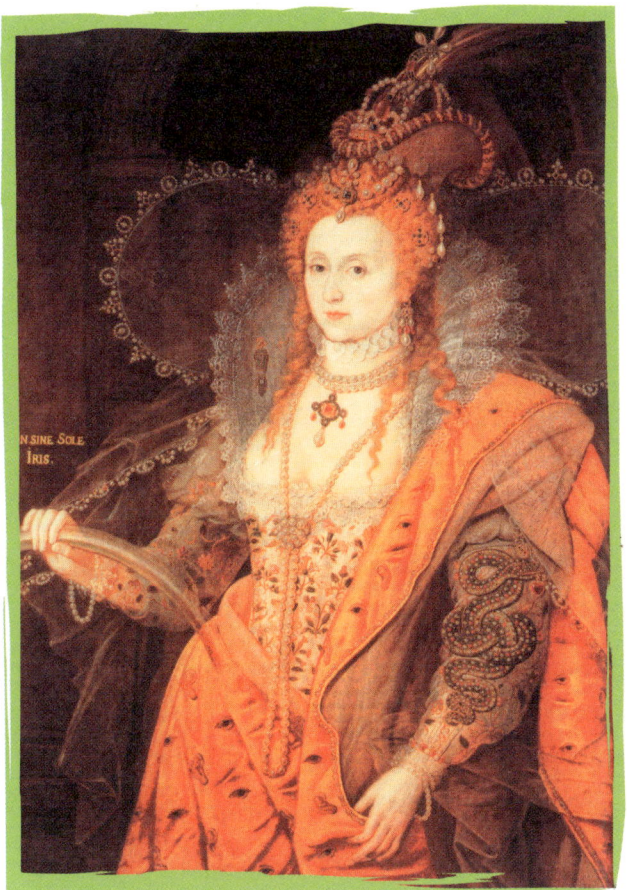

The 'rainbow' portrait of Queen Elizabeth I. Part of the
gown she is wearing here became an altar cloth at a
rural church in Herefordshire.

CLIMBING ROSE
'GLORIANA'
IN YOUR GARDEN

Award-winning rose breeder Chris Warner specialises in miniature climbers and 'Gloriana', launched in 1997, is one of his most popular, a vigorous climber with good-looking blackspot-resistant foliage.

Reaching a height of up to 3m (10ft), masses of lightly fragranced, magenta-purple blooms are produced almost from the top of the plant to the bottom over a long flowering season. All it asks in return is a position in full sun, facing in any direction except north and, given judicious feeding, it will thrive in any type of soil.

This makes it an ideal candidate for covering an ugly wall or fence but it will also grace a doorway most invitingly and scramble charmingly over a pillar or archway.

Be aware, though, that if you are growing it next to a wall, it will need support and the soil tends to be dry here so it will need plenty of water. The pruning of established plants in early spring is also recommended.

David Austin Roses, Bowling Green Lane, Albrighton, Wolverhampton, WV7 2HB. Tel: 01902 376 328.
Email: help@davidaustinroses.co.uk. www.davidaustinroses.co.uk.
See also: The Rose Society UK. www.therosesociety.org.uk.

Gloriana (Queen Elizabeth I)

If you happen to look up 'Gloriana' in any research resource you'll find plenty of references to this most 'glorious' of names. It is given to a genus of moths, an American country music group, an opera by the English composer Benjamin Britten and a royal barge – and these are just a few examples. But the very first time the name occurs is in one of the longest poems in the English language, *The Faerie Queene* by Edmund Spenser (1552-1599).

This epic poem is an allegorical fantasy first published in 1590, when Queen Elizabeth I was on the throne of England. Elizabeth was the daughter of the infamous King Henry VIII by Anne Boleyn, the second of his six unfortunate wives. Despite the tribulations of her father's reign, which included the dissolution of the catholic monasteries and bitter religious conflict, Elizabeth's reign was comparatively peaceful and positive. Edmund Spenser, a committed Protestant, ardently admired his queen and not only did he dedicate his poem to her but, in it, he portrayed her as Gloriana, The Faerie Queene herself. He even praised the Tudor dynasty, making dubious claims about Elizabeth's descent, through her great, great grandfather Owen Tudor, to King Arthur and the ancient kings of Britain. In an allegorical context, the poem follows the exploits of several noble knights in their individual quests for virtue.

The delighted Queen Elizabeth immediately granted Spenser a pension of £50 a year.

The reign of the first Elizabeth coincided with the golden age of British culture: literature, theatre and the arts blossomed during this period, as did technology, science and exploration. It was an age of prosperity and at the centre of it all, Elizabeth ruled as queen for almost forty-five years with – as she herself put it – 'the heart and stomach of a king'. She never married and, though she enjoyed a close relationship with Robert Dudley, First Earl of Leicester, she was known as the Virgin Queen.

The assertion of the Queen's virginity endured and is unexpectedly substantiated in the little early thirteenth-century church of St. Faith's in the Herefordshire village of Bacton, near the Welsh border. This had been the home of Blanche Parry, niece of Lady Troy, who brought up Elizabeth. Blanche became the Queen's life-long companion, the Chief Gentlewoman of the Queen's Most Honourable Privy Chamber and Keeper of Her Majesty's Jewels. In planning her retirement, Blanche had intended to return to her family's estate in Herefordshire and, to that end, she had commissioned a monument to herself at St. Faith's church, where several members of her family still lie interred in the family tomb. But things did not go according to plan and Blanche died in London, being buried at St. Margaret's Westminster. However, the monument remains at St. Faith's and is of great interest because, for the first time ever, it depicts Queen Elizabeth I iconically as *Gloriana* with Blanche kneeling in front of her. Perhaps to emphasise her closeness to the Queen, and perhaps even to confirm Elizabeth's virginity, part of Blanche's chosen inscription for the monument reads ... 'With maiden Queen a maide did end my life.' The church's original altar cloth, too, has been authenticated as having been made of fabric from the gown worn by Elizabeth in the famous 'rainbow' portrait of her.

Gloriana endures as a popular name and Queen Elizabeth II named the royal row barge *Gloriana* in honour of her predecessor and as a lasting legacy to mark her own Diamond Jubilee in 2012. Celebrations of the event included a glorious pageant on the River Thames involving a thousand boats. The *Gloriana*, with four state trumpeters astern, led the entire flotilla. In future, she will be retained as a charitable trust, used to promote better use of London's famous river and also as a means of encouraging people, especially young people, to engage with the sport of rowing.

BUSH ROSE
'GRACE DE MONACO'

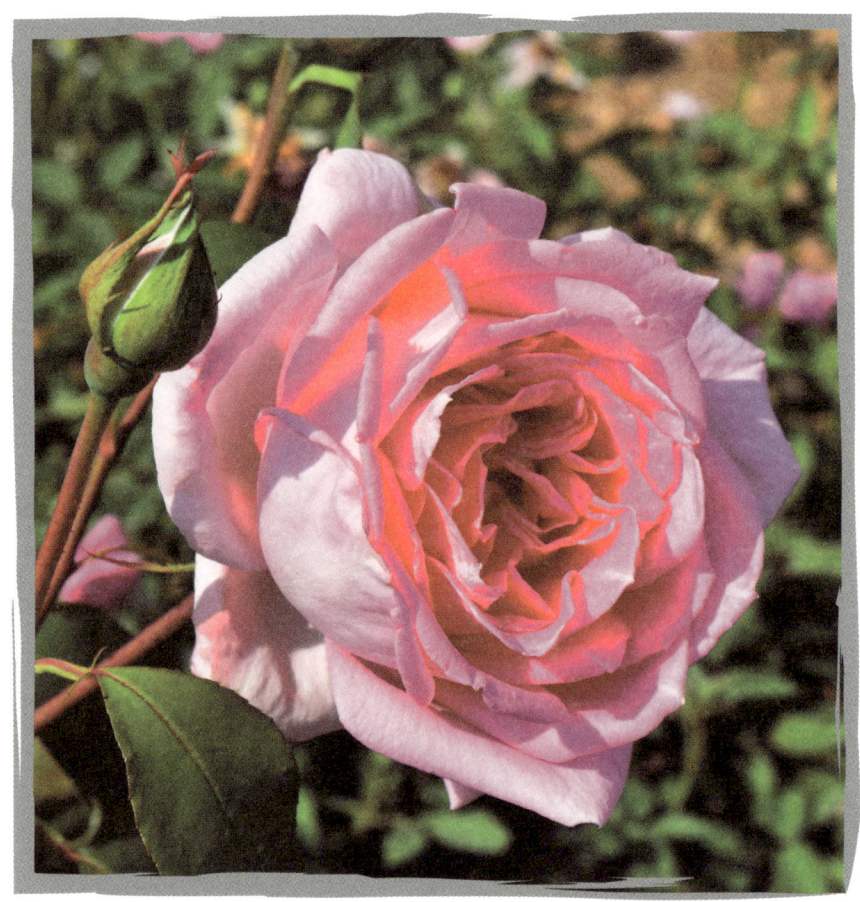

© Peter Beales Roses

Grace Kelly

1929-1982

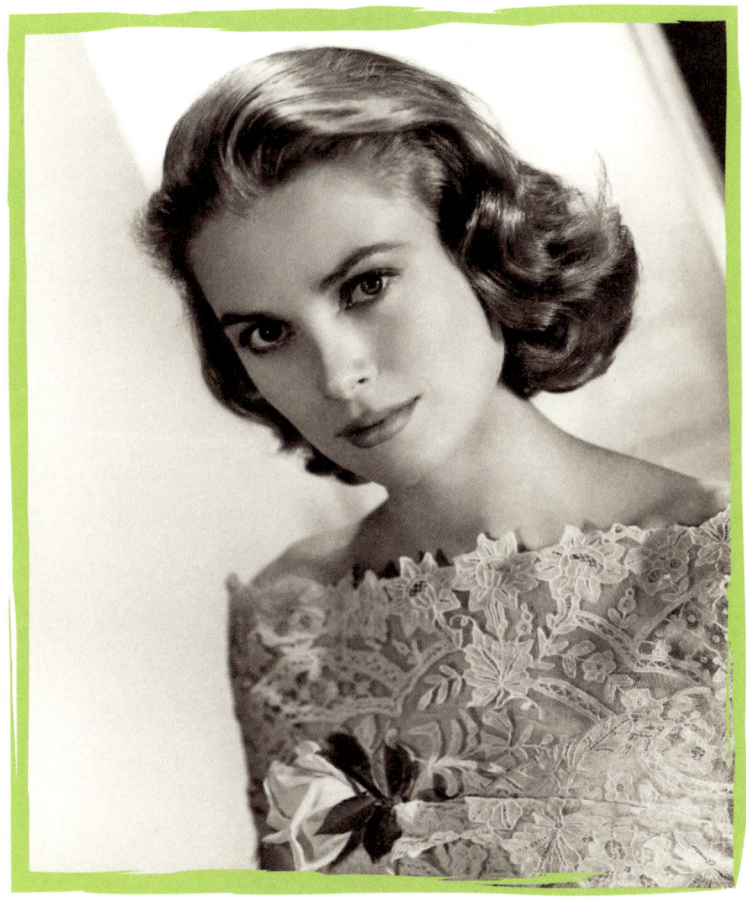

Rarely was a girl so appropriately named. Grace Kelly
epitomised elegance and refinement.

BUSH ROSE
'GRACE DE MONACO'
IN YOUR GARDEN

This lovely hybrid tea rose is as elegant as its namesake. Its bushy growth makes it equally at home in the rose bed or in a roomy pot on the patio.

Its delightful double blooms of light pink are fragrant and it will flower repeatedly throughout the season, reaching an eventual height of 90cm (3ft). Hybrid tea roses are easily recognised by their large flowers and pointed buds and are often what people first visualise when they think about roses.

Unlike floribunda roses, which produce clusters of flowers, hybrid tea roses tend to produce just a single flower on the end of each stem, which makes them versatile companions for other flowers in the vase.

They have a long flowering period, from early summer until the first frosts of autumn, and will always benefit from annual pruning and regular feeding with a good rose fertilizer in early spring and early summer, boosted by fortnightly liquid feeds throughout the flowering period.

Peter Beales Roses Ltd, London Road, Attleborough, Norwich, Norfolk, NR17 1AY, United Kingdom. Tel: +44 (0)1953 454707. www.classicroses.co.uk/roses. See also: The British Association of Rose Breeders. www.rosesuk.com.

Grace Kelly

It's probably impossible to find a bad photograph of Grace Kelly because she was quite simply a strikingly beautiful woman. The camera loved her and this, coupled with the fact that she was also a gifted, intelligent actress, meant that she enjoyed a stellar career in Hollywood. Her life story reads like a fairy tale because she even won the heart of a prince, but far from being a poor little Cinderella, Grace Patricia Kelly was born into the family of a wealthy American industrialist in Philadelphia, USA, in November 1929 and given every advantage her millionaire father could afford.

Both her parents were athletes; her father had won three Olympic gold medals for sculling and was President Roosevelt's National Director of Physical Fitness during WWII. Her mother taught Physical Education and was an athletics coach. Perhaps this was why Grace possessed an unconscious physical grace and was a natural dancer. She certainly danced and acted her way through school and began to dream of a stage career, winning a place at the American Academy of Dramatic Arts in New York. In a curious glimpse into the future, her graduation performance was as Tracy Lord, the socialite heiress who is the main character in *The Philadelphia Story*. It was a gift of a part for a young woman who was a Philadelphia socialite in real life.

Early successes were mainly on stage but it was her later work in television drama which led to her first film appearance in an unremarkable cameo role in the 1951 motion picture *Fourteen Hours*. One of the visitors to the set during filming was the actor Gary Cooper who found her very charming and, though she didn't seem destined for a movie career after this inauspicious beginning, it's probable that Gary Cooper had mentioned her to the producer Stanley Kramer because he offered her a starring role opposite Cooper in what was to become the landmark movie *High Noon*.

This set her on the meteoric path to stardom. Under contract to Metro-Goldwyn-Meyer, she was soon racking up credits in films which became classics. *Mogambo* was the first of these, in which she starred again with Cooper and won a Golden Globe Award for Best Supporting Actress. It was the first of many such accolades. Of her eleven films, three were for the same director, Alfred Hitchcock. They included Dial *M for Murder*, *Rear Window* and *To Catch a Thief* which was set on the French Riviera. And it was while leading the US delegation at the Cannes Film Festival in 1955 that Grace met Prince Rainier III, sovereign of the Principality of Monaco. By December of the same year, the prince had proposed to her. She accepted and, while making her last film in Hollywood, in which she played a young woman about to be married, she wore her own engagement ring. In an eerie echo of her earliest ambitions, her role was that of Tracy Lord and the film was *High Society*, a musical adaptation of *The Philadelphia Story*.

On April 19th 1956, in a lavish ceremony and wearing a gown made in Hollywood by an MGM designer, Grace Kelly became Princess Grace of Monaco, watched by a worldwide television audience of thirty million. The couple had three children, Caroline, Albert and Stéphanie and, during her marriage, Princess Grace was very active in charitable and cultural work, particularly in support of arts and children's charities. After her untimely death, Prince Rainier established the Princess Grace Foundation-USA to continue the work she had done anonymously in assisting young American artists working in dance, film and theatre. It has distributed more than $7 million to date.

Princess Grace lost her life as the result of an accident on a steep, winding mountain road above Monaco in September 1982 when her car failed to take a corner and plunged 120ft down a steep mountainside. Doctors said that she had suffered a mild stroke at the wheel. Her funeral was held at St. Nicholas Cathedral in Monaco, where she had been married twenty-six years earlier.

CLEMATIS ALPINA
'JACQUELINE DU PRÉ'

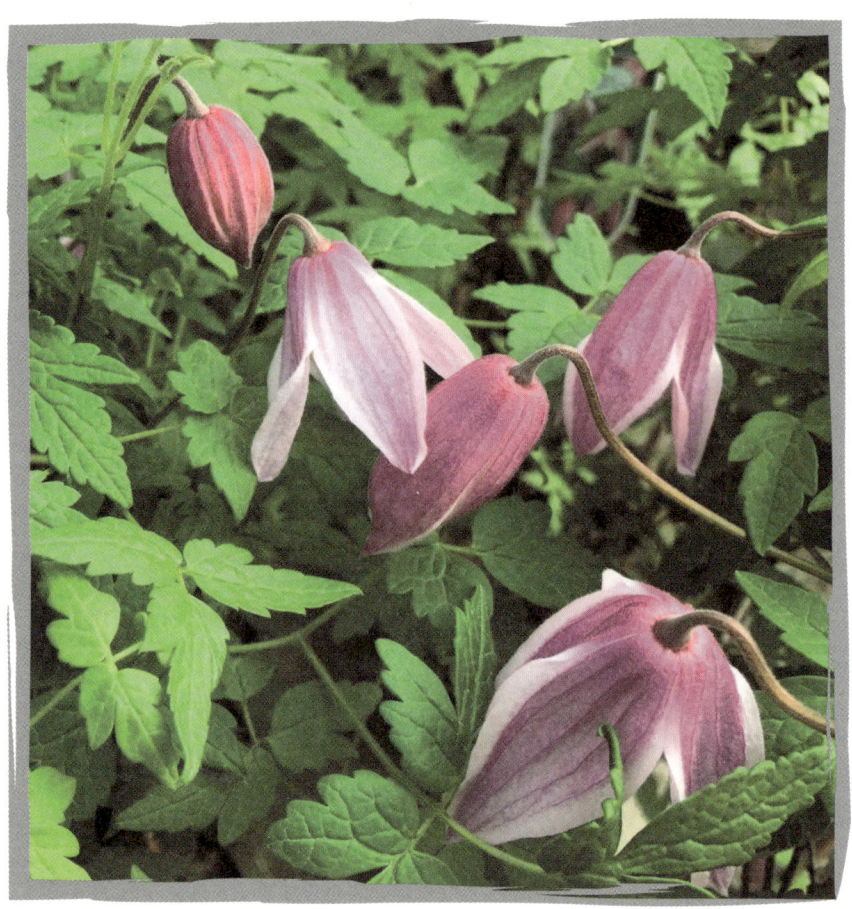

© Taylors Clematis

Jacqueline du Pré

1945-1987

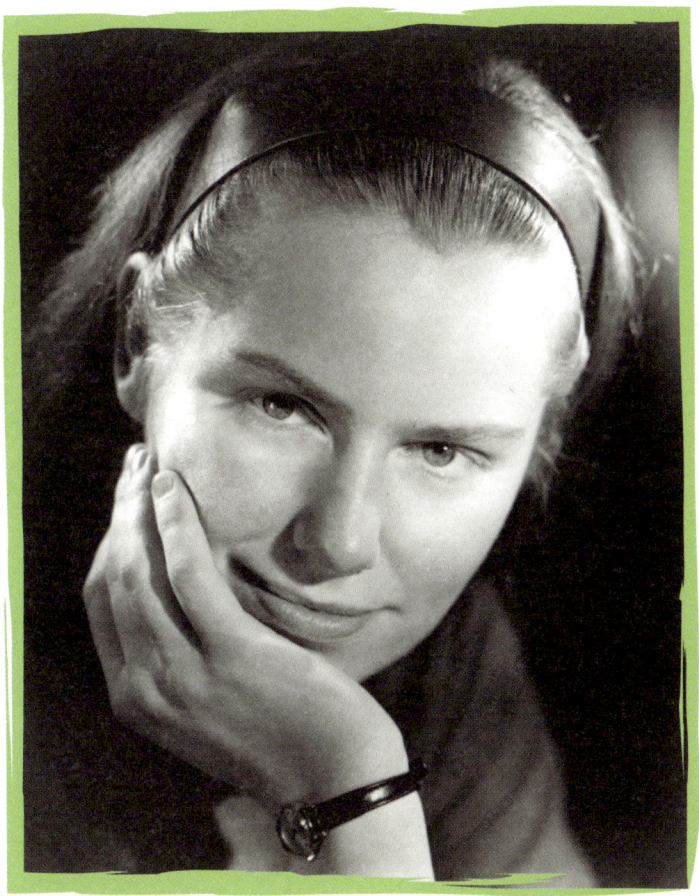

Jacqueline du Pré, a child prodigy in the classical mould.

CLEMATIS ALPINA
'JACQUELINE DU PRÉ'
IN YOUR GARDEN

A climber and a scrambler which will tolerate quite extreme conditions, Clematis *alpina* 'Jacqueline du Pré' asks nothing more than a moist but well-drained soil in order to produce a typical inflorescence of warm pink or rosy mauve threaded with slightly darker veins.

Distinctively, its tepals are longer than most other alpinas by about 1.3cm (½in), and have a conspicuous white or 'silvery' edging that gives them a sharp outline, accentuating the points.

The fine harmony of colours might be lost on us if the flowers were given to weeping (as some excellent alpinas are). Instead, the nodding bells on stems like a shepherd's crook are so free that they can turn outward and even upward here and there and open nearly flat as they mature, attracting bees and butterflies. So in full bloom in the spring, 'Jacqueline du Pré' can be one of the most eye-catching of all clematis.

Taylors Clematis, Sutton Road, Sutton, Doncaster, South Yorkshire, DN6 9JZ. Tel: 01302 700716. Email: info@taylorsclematis.co.uk. www.taylorsclematis.co.uk. See also: The British Clematis Society. www.britishclematis.org.uk.

Jacqueline du Pré

Born in Oxford of an English mother and a father whose family hailed from Jersey in the Channel Islands, the British cellist Jacqueline Mary du Pré blazed across the firmament of classical music in Britain and America like a bright comet for twelve years between 1961 and 1973, lighting up international concert platforms with her passionate performances and her technical brilliance. The story is told that at the age of four, while she was listening to the BBC radio programme *Children's Hour*, she first heard the sound of the cello and immediately asked to have 'one of those'. Her mother, the pianist Iris du Pré, was pleased to buy little Jackie a cello for her fifth birthday and she set about composing simple pieces for her daughter to play. But Jacqueline didn't need them for long; she took to the instrument immediately. They might have been made for each other.

Jacqueline came to the attention of the concert-going public at a very young age, entering and winning local competitions. At the age of ten, she embarked on a course of study with the distinguished cellist William Pleeth at London's Guildhall School of Music and he wrote of her: '...*I am of the opinion that she will have a great career.*' He was right. By the time she was fifteen, in 1960, she had won the Guildhall's prestigious Gold Medal and in the same year she was awarded the Queen's Prize for young British musicians under thirty. These were the first of many honours, fellowships and doctorates which were heaped upon her during her lifetime, including an OBE.

A debut recital at London's Wigmore Hall is almost a rite of passage for any aspiring young solo instrumentalist and it's always seen as a challenge. Jacqueline's debut was a resounding success and effectively launched her career with many offers of concerts and broadcasts. She was just seventeen years old when, in 1962, she created a sensation at the Royal Festival Hall with her performance of the Elgar Cello Concerto with the BBC Symphony Orchestra. She performed the same demanding show piece the following year at the Proms and her performance won her so many fans that she was asked to repeat it for the following three years in succession, conducted each time by Sir Malcolm Sargent. Since then she has always been associated with the Elgar Concerto and her interpretation of it remains the benchmark to which others aspire.

For the best part of the next decade, du Pré was at the height of her career. A tour of North America and Canada in 1965 with the BBC Symphony Orchestra sealed her transatlantic reputation and the critics almost ran out of superlatives in reviewing her performances. Her playing, described as 'impassioned' and 'elemental', was always technically brilliant. Her recording of the Elgar Concerto in 1965 became an instant best-seller and remains one to this day.

In 1966 she met the young Argentine-born Israeli conductor and pianist Daniel Barenboim and in 1967, after Jacqueline's conversion to Judaism, they were married in Israel. The Barenboims were the golden couple of the classical musical world, an exuberant and spontaneous partnership which resulted in definitive performances of many works by a whole host of composers, both on the concert platform and in the recording studio. They were often joined in these by friends and contemporaries who were also fine instrumentalists in their own right, Pinchas Zukerman, Itzak Perlman and Zubin Metha among them. Jacqueline du Pré had the musical world at her feet.

By 1971, Jacqueline had begun experiencing a sensation of numbness in her hands, and her playing began to be affected by it. Extensive tests in 1973 showed that she was suffering from multiple sclerosis and her health deteriorated rapidly. By 1976 she was largely confined to a wheelchair and, though she managed a little teaching, she never played in public again. Jacqueline du Pré died at her London home, aged just forty-two, in 1987.

CLIMBING FUCHSIA
'LADY BOOTHBY'

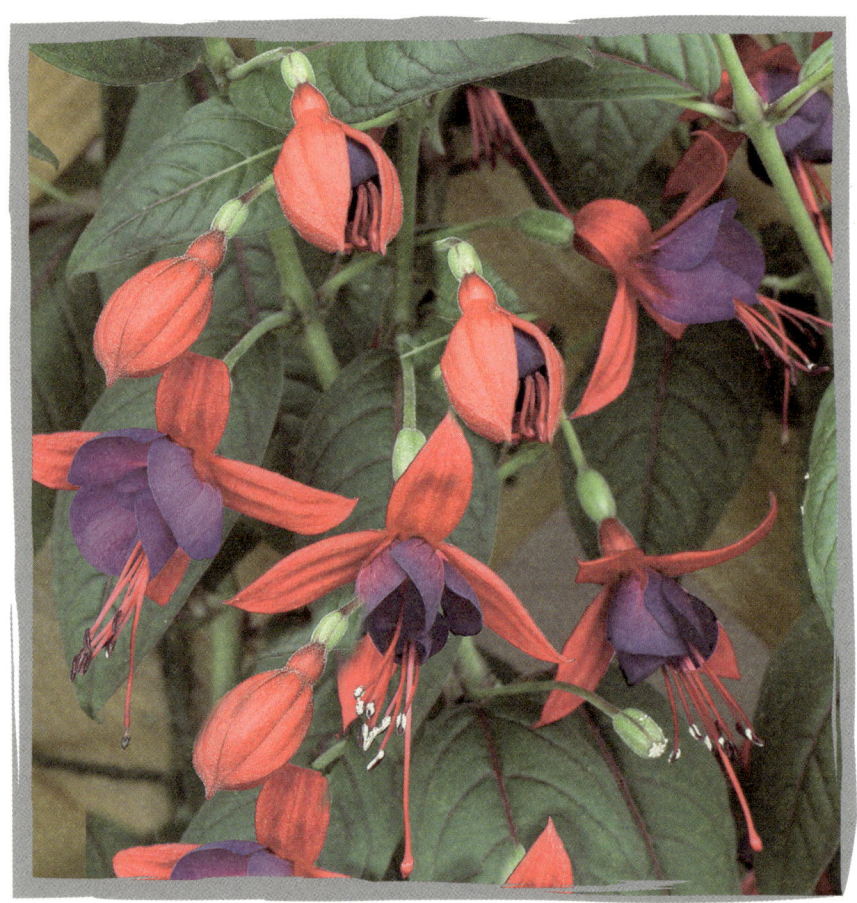

© Volmary Ltd

Lady Boothby

1878–1969

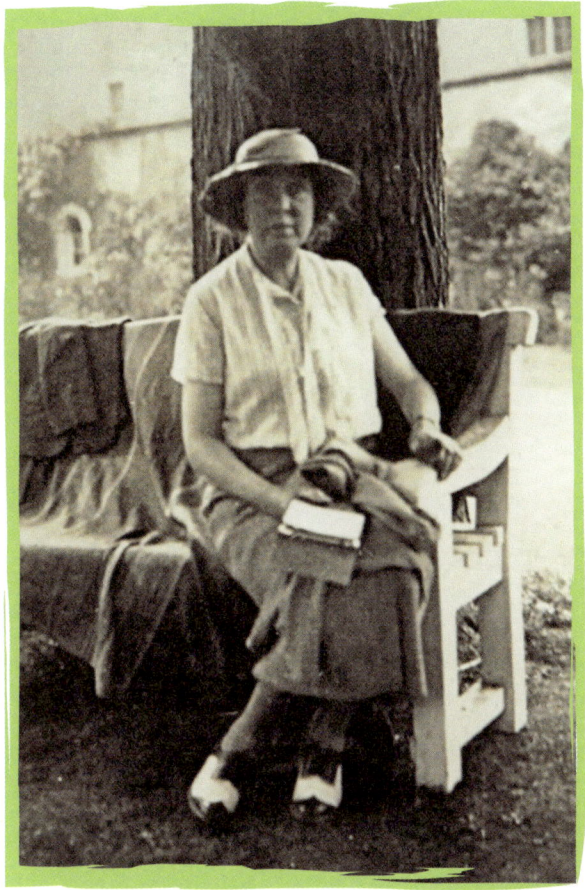

Lady Boothby in the grounds of Fonmon Castle:
an informal picture from the family album,
by kind permission.

CLIMBING FUCHSIA
'LADY BOOTHBY'
IN YOUR GARDEN

'Lady Boothby' is a stunning addition to the border or patio, a beautiful fuchsia which is a true climbing variety. Grow against a wall, a pergola or within a frame in a patio pot.

Easily reaching a height of over 100cm (3ft-4ft) it will need support but will reward the gardener with an abundance of fabulous reddish-purple flowers throughout the summer, particularly if regularly dead-headed and thoughtfully watered.

'Lady Boothby' is fully hardy and will continue to give pleasure year after year though it does benefit from a hard annual pruning in spring, down to just above where the new shoots are appearing. Keep an eye on it when growth begins, tying in and pinching back where appropriate.

It will benefit from a dressing of general fertilizer in spring and again later in the summer. Other than this, it is relatively undemanding, thriving in full sun or semi-shade in a fertile, well-drained soil or in balanced compost. Cuttings are best taken in the autumn.

J. Parker Dutch Bulbs Ltd, 14 Hadfield Street, Old Trafford, Manchester, M16 9FG. Tel: 0161-848-1100. www.jparkers.co.uk. See also: The British Fuchsia Society. www.thebfs.org.uk.

Lady Boothby

Clara Boothby was, in many ways, a reluctant aristocrat, having come into possession of Fonmon Castle, the family seat in the Vale of Glamorgan, entirely by accident. She had been born a Valpy, her father being a member of the distinguished family of educationalists who hailed originally from Jersey. Clara's mother was the sister of Oliver Henry Jones, the last male heir of the family which owned Fonmon Castle. When, in 1906, Clara married Hugo Boothby, the young couple had no expectation of inheriting either the baronetcy on his side, or the historic family home on hers since, between them, they had a total of six older siblings. However, the Great War and various illnesses effectively culled the ranks and the couple eventually found themselves in possession of both the Boothby family title and a rather lovely old castle in Wales.

When Sir Hugo and Lady Clara Boothby arrived at Fonmon in 1933, it was literally falling down and there was no money for repairs. Still, they did their best and though their work on the castle was severely affected by the deprivations of the Second World War, Clara was able to bring her great love of gardening to bear on the estate. She was particularly keen on fuchsias, an enthusiasm she shared with her friend HRH Queen Mary and the story is told that while the Queen was visiting Fonmon in 1938, the two of them spotted an announcement in the local Welsh newspaper publicising a meeting of FUCHSIA. After some discussion, they decided that, really, such a society should be supported if it was dedicated to the development of their favourite flower. Lady Boothby duly approached the organisation which was holding the meeting, only to discover that the name was an acronym for Friendship, Usefulness, Cheerfulness, Helpfulness, Sympathy, Instruction and Amusement and that these were the declared aims of the Women's Conservative Association. Since members of the Royal family are not permitted to associate with any political party, Queen Mary had to bow out at that point but the idea of a British Fuchsia Society had been born and, appropriately, it grew from there. Lady Clara Boothby went on to become its first President and, in her opening President's Address to the Society in 1938, she made a point of thanking the Head Gardeners of many old country houses for their help in sourcing fuchsia varieties which had fallen out of favour. These were then cultivated and the BFS went on to distribute the plants among its members. It was only natural that a fuchsia should be named in her honour and the vigorous cultivar 'Lady Boothby' is distinguished in being one of the few climbing varieties.

The presidency of the British Fuchsia Society was the only public office which Lady Boothby ever held simply because she was profoundly deaf as the result of a childhood illness. To her great regret, this disability curtailed any charitable work she might otherwise have undertaken.

Lady Boothby was also rather shy and, though the walls of her elegant home were hung with inherited family portraits by Sir Joshua Reynolds and other distinguished artists, the only pictures which exist of her are three fading family snapshots, one of which appears here by kind permission of her grandson, Sir Brooke Boothby Bt., who also lists 'gardening' as his hobby. He remembers his grandmother with great affection as 'a mischievous soul with a great sense of humour' and her absorbing hobby was all the more enjoyable because it was unaffected by her deafness. There was nothing self-important about Lady Boothby and she never minded getting her hands dirty. Sir Brooke recalls that one of his clearest childhood memories is that of his much-loved grandmother on her knees among her flowerbeds – weeding.

HOSTA
'LADY ISOBEL BARNETT'

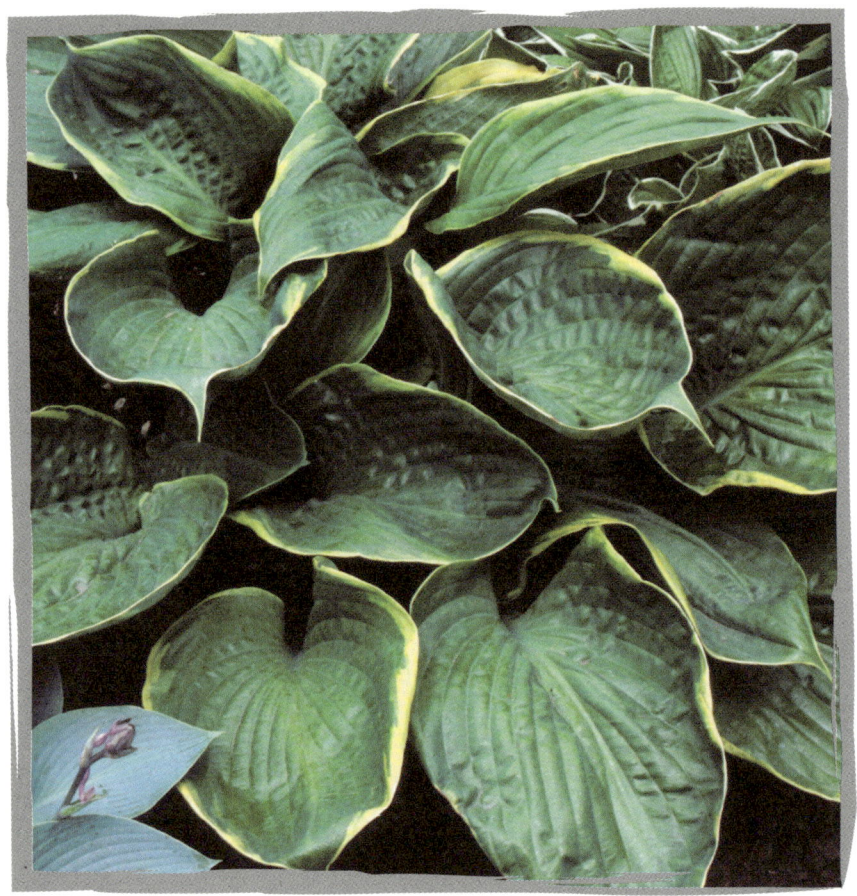

© Tim Saville

Lady Isobel Barnett

1918–1980

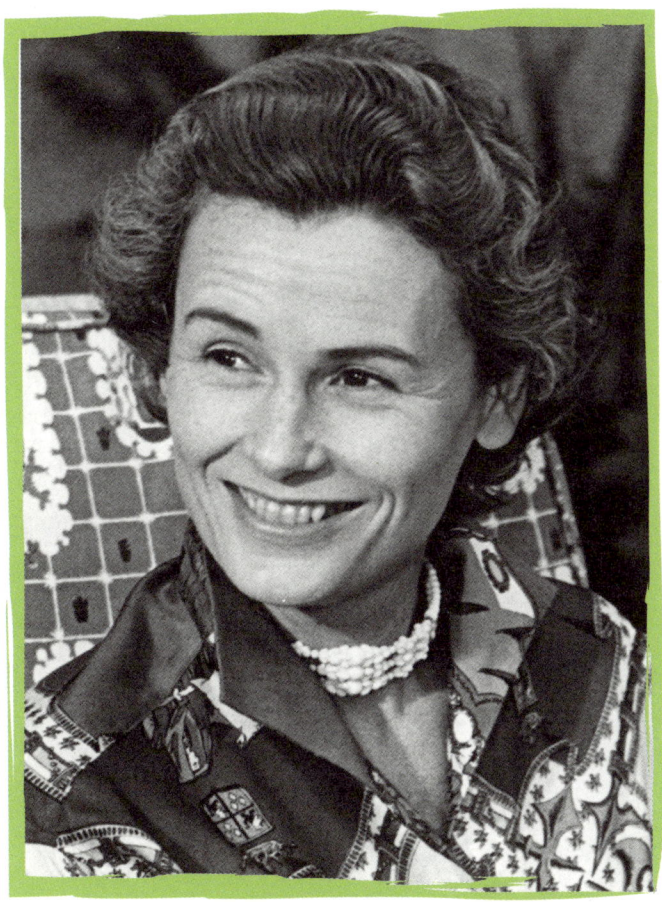

Isobel Barnett, the most ladylike of early television
personalities.

HOSTA
'LADY ISOBEL BARNETT'
IN YOUR GARDEN

Lady Isobel Barnett herself was a great fan of hostas, particularly for shaded areas of the garden, and it was while listening to her talking about them on the radio that Diana Grenfell – who had never previously heard of hostas – became intrigued.

Diana went on to become an eminent horticulturalist, specialising in these lovely, hardy perennials and was awarded the prestigious RHS Veitch Memorial Medal. When she created this delightful hosta in 1996, she had no hesitation in naming it after the woman who had been her inspiration.

The chief criticism of hostas is that they are irresistible to molluscs but they don't need to be. Diana suggests spraying with a ten per cent solution of garlic juice early in the season.

Then, towards summer, a ten per cent solution of household ammonia on its own, or with the garlic, is recommended. Using ammonia too early will scorch the leaves. There's plenty of information on successful hosta growing on the website of the British Hosta and Hemerocallis Society.

Fransen Hostas, Paradijsweg 5, 2461 TK Ter Aar, Netherlands, Europe. Tel: +31 172 602 031. www.hostaparadise.com. See also: The British Hosta and Hemerocallis Society. www.hostahem.org.uk.

Lady Isobel Barnett

The name of Lady Isobel Barnett was one of the best known in Britain during the 1950s and 60s because her career coincided with the rapid post-war growth in popularity of the BBC's television service. Regular panel games and quiz shows like *What's My Line?* were the staples of the television schedules, drawing huge audiences, and the celebrity panellists would also appear on popular radio programmes like *Any Questions?*, *Many a Slip* and the all-woman panel show *Petticoat Line*. One of the most enduringly popular celebrities associated with these programmes was Lady Isobel Barnett who, with her grace, elegance, knowledge and wit, seemed to be the quintessential embodiment of what viewers and listeners thought of as being typical of the English aristocracy. But this was quite far from the truth.

Isobel Morag Marshall was Scottish, born in Aberdeen in 1918 to a local doctor and his wife. It seemed natural that she should follow in her father's footsteps and Isobel Marshall qualified as a doctor in 1940 at Glasgow University. In 1941, she married solicitor and company director Geoffrey Barnett and took up a post as an obstetrician in Leicestershire. Their son was born in 1944 and Isobel became a magistrate thereafter. In 1952, Geoffrey Barnett was elected Chairman of Leicester City Council and its ceremonial Lord Mayor and it was at the end of his year of office in 1953 that the whole of the eastern seaboard of Britain was hit by a flood of biblical proportions – than 300 people lost their lives. The Lord Mayor of Leicester had worked tirelessly in raising money for flood relief and, as a result, he was knighted for political and public services, becoming Sir Geoffrey Barnett. His wife acquired the courtesy title of Lady Barnett. It was in the same year that she made her first appearance on television as one of the panel of *What's My Line?*. She was an instant hit.

There followed nearly two decades of exhilarating fame. Suddenly, Lady Barnett's charming smile was everywhere, particularly on television and radio. With her erudition and elegance, she was a 'natural'. She was invited to open shops and exhibitions and, with her crystal-clear voice and witty presentation, she was constantly in demand as an after-dinner speaker. It seemed her fame would know no bounds, but the style of television programmes began to undergo a subtle change and they became more informal. Then, in the voracious way that television has of exploiting personalities and celebrities until the next and newest sensation comes along, the invitations began to dwindle. One long-running series after another came to an end and the public began to see less and less of Lady Isobel Barnett. There was no longer any demand for her kind of broadcasting.

Lady Barnett took it badly. Her husband had died in 1970, and she eventually retired and retreated to her home in the village of Cossington in Leicestershire. Here she began to live a reclusive and increasingly eccentric life, not seeing anyone and only occasionally venturing out to buy food from the village grocer's shop. It was this that led to her last sensational public appearance in 1980, this time in court for shoplifting. She had stolen a can of tuna and a carton of cream, together valued at just 87 pence, and the police were called. In court, she was fined £76 for the offence. What made her do it? She had enough money and certainly didn't need to steal, so perhaps it was an unconscious cry for help. Whatever the reason, she found the shame too much to bear and took her own life four days later. It was a deeply sad and ignominious end to a life of so much promise and fulfilment. In Cossington village, a short new road has been named Barnett Close in her memory.

AURICULA
'LUCY LOCKET'

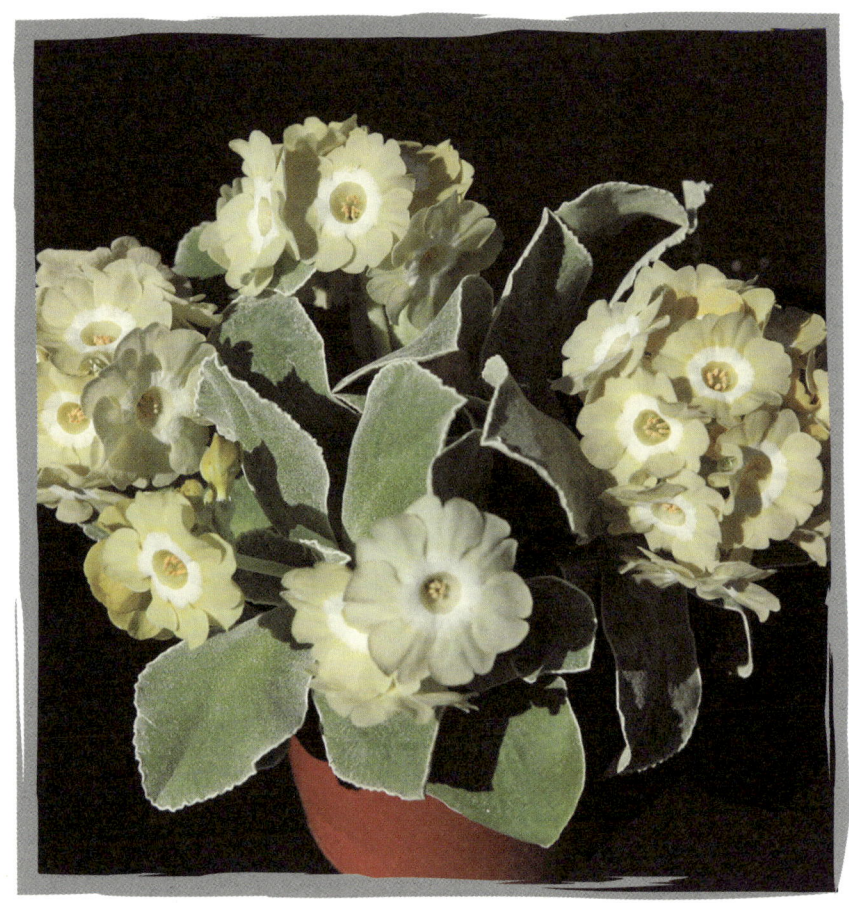

© Drointon Nurseries

Lucy Locket

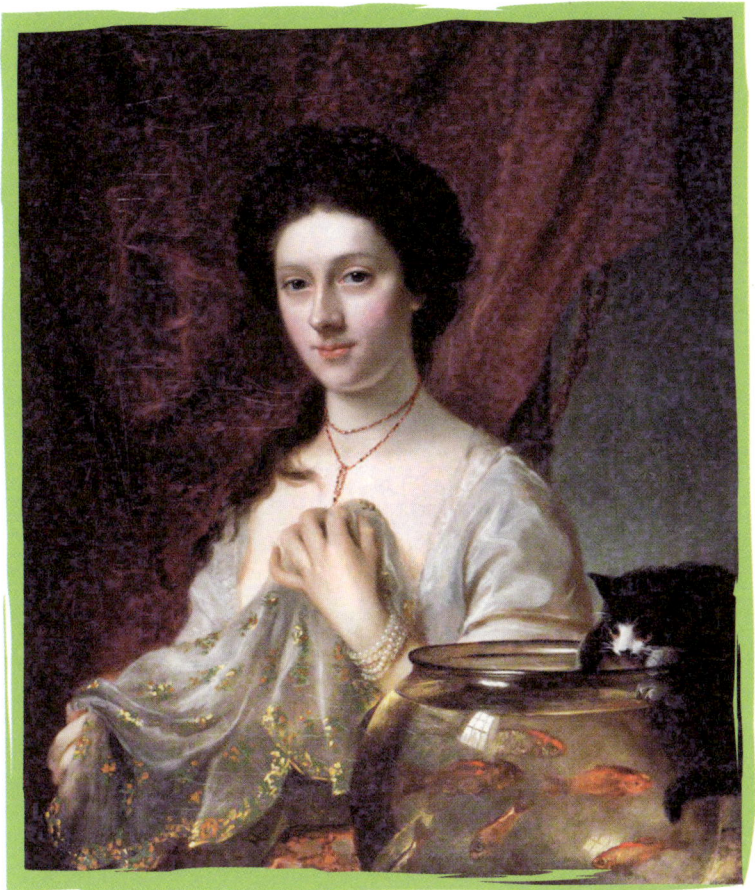

This is certainly not a portrait of Lucy Locket and no one knows what Lucy looked like; it is a portrait of Catherine Maria (Kitty) Fischer by Nathaniel Hone. With wry humour, the artist has painted a second 'kitty' in the bottom right hand corner of the painting and she, too, is 'fishing'.

AURICULA
'LUCY LOCKET'
IN YOUR GARDEN

The plant name is a diminutive of the Latin *auris*, meaning 'an ear', because its leaves are said to resemble little bears' ears. Many are grown in pots but 'Lucy Locket' is a true 'border' auricula and thrives outside in a well-drained position. Growth begins in late February, gaining momentum during March. Flowers emerge towards the middle of April and they are at their best throughout the following month.

Once flowering is over, however, the plant goes into a rapid decline and growth stops. Auriculas are not happy in high summer so it's wise to give them some shade, but resist the temptation to over-water because the plant is only using water for survival during the months it dislikes.

Things cheer up again in September and, if the shading is removed, the occasional plant will start to flower again. Dormant during the winter, they are completely hardy and will come to no harm in a heavy frost, emerging once again towards the end of February to greet a brand new spring.

Drointon Nurseries, Plaster Pitts, Norton Conyers, Ripon, North Yorkshire, HG4 5EF. Tel: 01765 641 849. Email: info@auricula-plants.co.uk. www.auricula-plants.co.uk. See also: The National Auricula & Primula Society UK. www.auriculaandprimula.org.uk.

Lucy Locket

Surely, there was no such person! Yes, there probably was, because nursery rhymes very often make reference to living people and events in history. For example...

> *'Ring-a-ring-a-rosies,*
> *A pocketful of posies,*
> *A-tishoo! A-tishoo!*
> *We all fall down.'*

...is still being sung by today's children though it dates from the Great Plague, which brought London to its knees in 1665. The rhyme describes the typical rosy-coloured, ring-shaped swellings of infected lymph nodes and a posy of flowers held to the nose was said to offer protection from infection. Sneezing and coughing occurred when the patient was near death. However, recent scholarly research entirely refutes this theory and it could well be that it is nothing more than a children's party game involving dancing in a circle. No one really knows.

But what about Lucy Locket? Well, Lucy herself was probably not making headlines in the broadside ballads of the eighteenth century but she's not the only girl referred to in the verse. Perhaps you remember the lines from childhood:

> *Lucy Locket lost her pocket*
> *Kitty Fisher found it*
> *N'er a penny was there in it*
> *Only ribbon round it.*

The famous diarist Samuel Pepys offers us a clue here. On April 23rd 1668 he wrote that he and an actress friend had been '... to the Cock Alehouse and drank and eat a lobster...' The Olde Cock Alehouse in London's Fleet Street has been the haunt of writers and journalists for nearly 500 years, popular ever since it was first built on an adjacent site in 1558. Though there is no written evidence to support the claim, it seems that during the eighteenth century, a hundred years after Pepys wrote his diaries, a young woman by the name of Lucy Locket worked there as a barmaid and she is the subject of the nursery rhyme. But how did Lucy manage to lose a pocket? What we have to remember is that the word has changed its meaning and, in Lucy's day, a 'pocket' was a bag or a pouch and it certainly wouldn't have had much in it from Lucy's small wages. Not a penny, in fact, when Kitty Fisher found it.

Kitty Fisher was as rich as Lucy Locket was poor. Catherine Maria Fischer, or 'Kitty', as she was popularly known, had become extremely wealthy by granting her physical favours to the upper classes. Born to a very poor family in 1741, Kitty first found employment as a milliner but soon her beauty caught the attention of some aristocratic young men-about-town and it wasn't long before she had been introduced into London high society. She took it by storm and soon became a scandalous courtesan. Rich men adored her but their wives loathed her.

Thanks to the gifts showered upon her by her wealthy lovers, Kitty Fisher became famous for her flamboyant lifestyle: liveried servants attended her, she spent money like water and she is said on one occasion to have eaten a £100 note on a slice of bread and butter. Painted by the most eminent portraitists of the day, she always dressed very expensively and was often seen wearing thousands of pounds worth of diamonds. So, in this contemporary ditty, the wags of Fleet Street were lampooning Kitty Fisher rather than poor, hard-working little Lucy Locket, who served them with their beer and could ill-afford to lose her pocket.

Kitty's flamboyant lifestyle couldn't last. Though she married well at the age of twenty-five to John Norris, son of the Member of Parliament for Rye, three months later she was 'in a decline' and died shortly afterwards in the arms of her distraught new husband. Her death was attributed to lead poisoning from her use of cosmetics, though she could well have died from consumption, but her fame as the most celebrated English courtesan of the eighteenth century lives on in the unlikely context of a nursery rhyme.

HYBRID TEA ROSE
'MADAM SPEAKER'

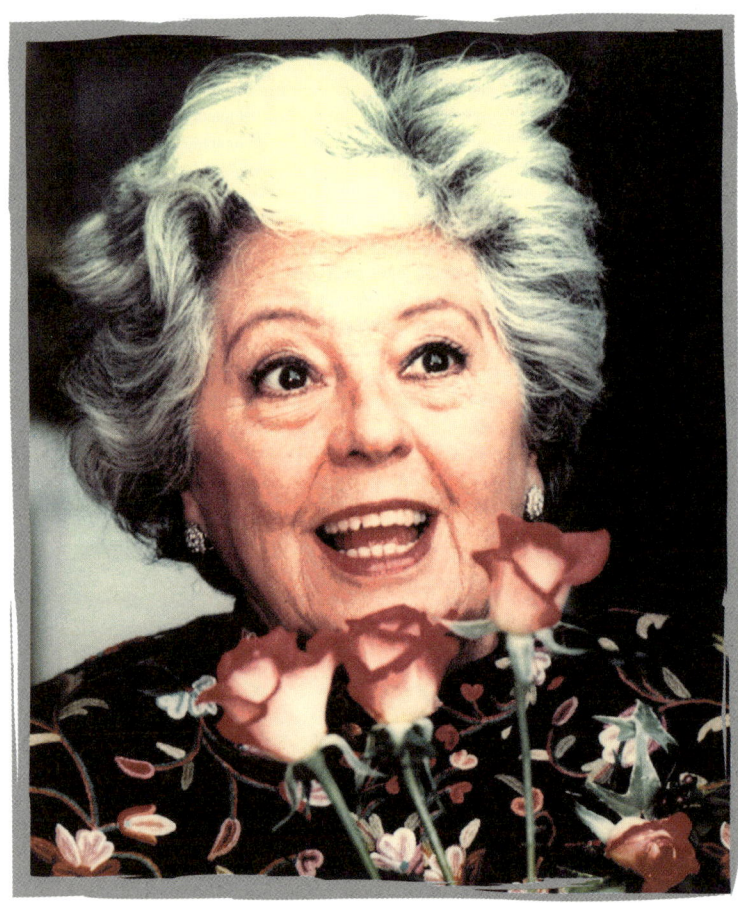

The only one of our 'Pretty Maids' who is actually holding the
flower named for her. From Baroness Boothroyd's private
collection by kind permission.

Madam Speaker (Betty Boothroyd)

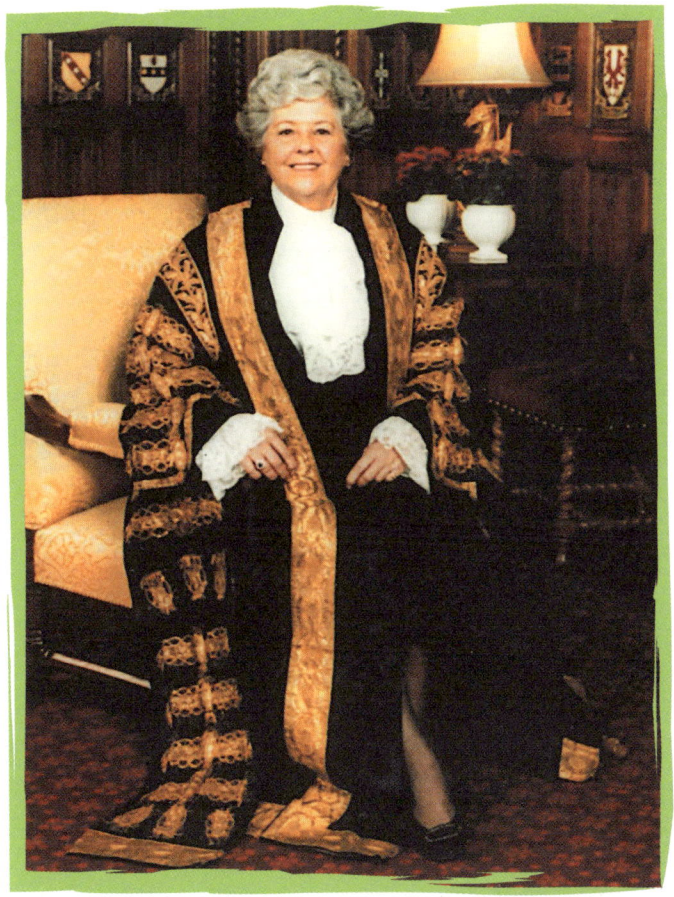

Madam Speaker in full parliamentary regalia –
except the wig!

HYBRID TEA ROSE
'MADAM SPEAKER'
IN YOUR GARDEN

The photograph on the previous page is of Labour MP Betty Boothroyd in 1992, soon after her election as the first ever woman to become Speaker of the House of Commons. To mark the occasion she was presented with the hybrid tea rose, named 'Madam Speaker' in her honour, by its grower, J.B. Turner of Wisbech. Delightedly sprinkling its roots with champagne, she said: 'I hope it will embody the characteristics every Speaker should have – hardy by nature, disease free, flourishing in all conditions, pleasing to the eye, fragrant to the senses and a pleasure to have around'.

To Baroness Boothroyd's great disappointment, this rose is no longer being commercially grown in the UK. However, the French grower Meilland produces the variety but it is sold under the name 'Bolchoi' and the breeder's reference (the varietal name) is Meizuzes. www.meilland.com

We're very grateful for this information which was provided by Roses UK, the marketing division of BARB (the British Association of Rose Breeders) which aims to maintain and increase the profile of the nation's favourite flower, the rose, through promotional activities. www.rosesuk.com.

And if your heart is set on finding a specific rose, then this web address could prove invaluable: www.rosesuk.com/roselocator.

Madam Speaker (Betty Boothroyd)

It was Sophocles who said that 'success is dependent upon effort' and no one has proved him right more than Betty Boothroyd, to give her the name by which everyone knows her.

The Rt. Hon. Baroness Boothroyd OM was born into a family of textile workers in a modest back-to-back house in Dewsbury, Yorkshire, on 8th October 1929. She received a state education at council schools, culminating in a place at the Dewsbury College of Commerce and Art before she changed horses in mid-stream during the 1940s and decided that she wanted to become a dancer. Typically, she worked hard at it and, blessed with a pretty face, long legs and a determined attitude, she won a coveted place in the well-known dancing troupe *The Tiller Girls,* but it didn't take her long to realise that show business was not for her. She had higher ideals in mind.

Betty Boothroyd had been a Labour Party member since her teenage years and she now turned her attention to the world of government. During the 1950s, she worked in the House of Commons as a political assistant to various Members of Parliament, including a fellow Yorkshire woman, the feisty socialist Barbara Castle. Visiting the United States in 1960 to witness the Kennedy campaign, Betty Boothroyd stayed on in Washington for two years, working as an assistant for an American congressman, before returning to pick up the threads of her work back in London.

The time had come to test the political waters for herself with the ultimate goal of winning a seat in Parliament. She began contesting elections, standing as a Parliamentary candidate four times before winning the seat for West Bromwich in 1973. She went on to represent that constituency for twenty-seven years and, from the very start, hers was a glittering parliamentary career. After her election to Westminster she became an assistant Government Whip, then a Member of the European parliament from 1975 to 1977. She was already a member of the Labour Party National Executive Committee and of the House of Commons Commission when she became a Deputy Speaker in 1987.

In 1992, Betty Boothroyd was elected Speaker of the House of Commons – the first woman ever to hold the office – with a majority of 134 votes over her nearest rival. However, she politely refused to wear the traditional Speaker's wig, a rather unattractive head-piece. She served as Speaker until her retirement in 2000 and was tireless in spreading the political message, even appearing as a special guest on the BBC children's television programme Live & Kicking in a bid to get youngsters interested in politics.

During her term of office as 'Madam Speaker', Betty Boothroyd served under two Prime Ministers, John Major until 1997 and

Tony Blair thereafter until 2000. Though of very different political persuasions, they both paid affectionate tributes to her when she stepped down from the role. John Major said she was an 'outstanding Speaker' while Tony Blair declared that she was 'something of a national institution'. She had been Chancellor of the Open University since 1995 and, with retirement, honours began to be heaped upon her. In 2009 she underwent major open-heart surgery in an NHS hospital, after which she was asked why she hadn't had the operation performed privately. She didn't hesitate before answering: 'I can afford private insurance but I won't do it'. This highly-principled woman had earned her privileges but she never abandoned her socialist beliefs.

In 2001 Betty Boothroyd, the ex-Tiller Girl, was created a Life Peer, taking the title Baroness Boothroyd of Sandwell, and in 2005 she was admitted to the Order of Merit, a special honour in the personal gift of the Queen and awarded to only twenty-four individuals of great achievement in their field. You can almost hear Sophocles cheering from the wings.

DAFFODIL
'MARIE CURIE'

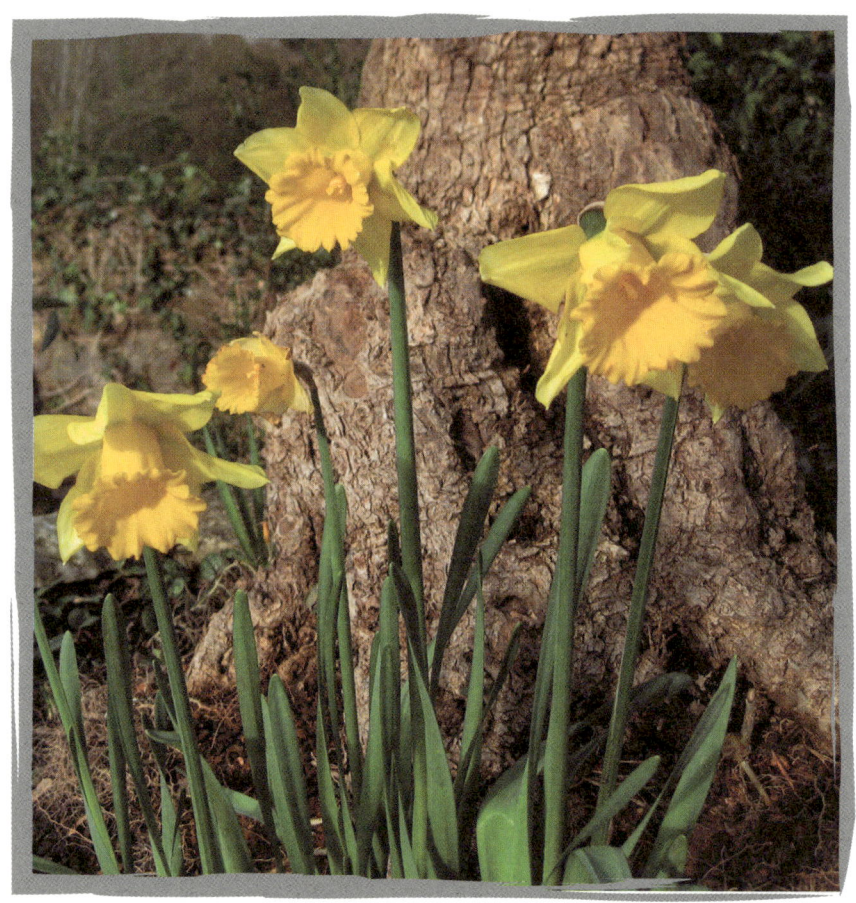

Daffodils in the author's garden.

Marie Curie

1867–1934

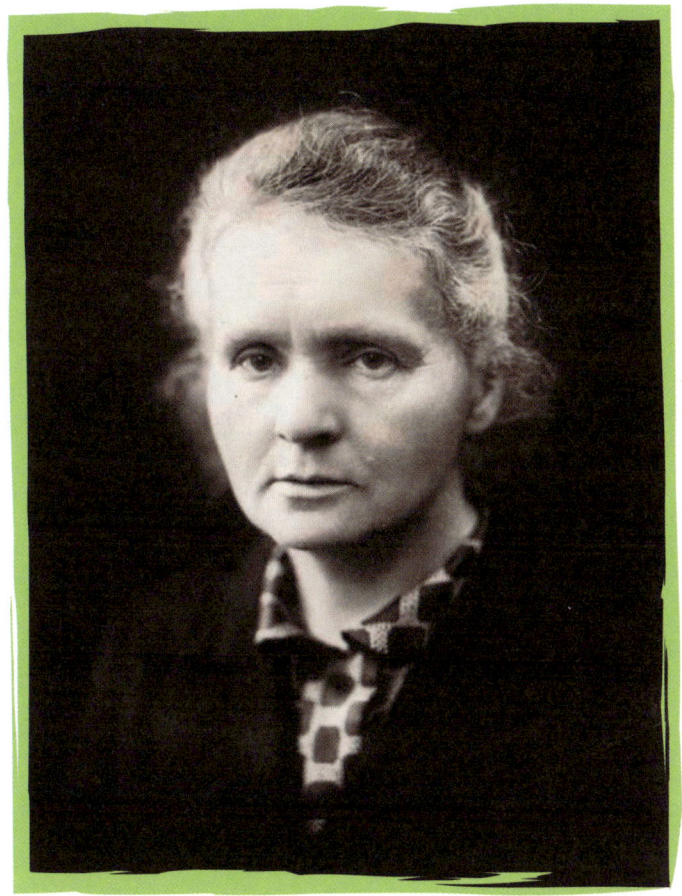

Marie Curie, circa 1920.

DAFFODIL
'MARIE CURIE'
IN YOUR GARDEN

A diligent search for bulbs of a daffodil specifically named 'Marie Curie' could lead to hours of frustration because, though the flower itself is so strongly associated with her name, there does not appear to be one. But with its bright yellow, trumpet-shaped flower, the much-loved, familiar daffodil is the ultimate herald of spring, new beginnings and new hope. Small wonder, then, that it has been chosen by the Marie Curie Charity as its symbol for the annual Great Daffodil Appeal. In this context, a search for a 'Marie Curie' daffodil would yield pictures of brooches, lapel pins and other charitable paraphernalia.

March is an appropriate month for the appeal because with the coming of spring, daffodils are growing profusely in woodland, gardens, through grass and under trees. Though incredibly simple to grow, daffodils will reward a little thought in the planting. Plant your bulbs in autumn, at least twice as deep as their height; a bulb that is 5cm (2in) tall will do best planted at a depth of 10cm (4in). Drainage is important too, particularly for container-grown bulbs. When planted directly into the ground, daffodils look really lovely growing in drifts and clumps where they will self-seed and naturalise. Planting large numbers of bulbs is made a lot easier by using a specific bulb planting tool. After flowering, allow the foliage to die back naturally.

Sutton's Ltd., Woodview Road, Paignton, Devon, TQ4 7NG.
Tel: Customer Services: 0333 043 0700. www.suttons.co.uk.
Please note that 10% of all Sutton's daffodil sales are given to support Marie Curie. See also: The Daffodil Society. www.thedaffodilsociety.com.

Marie Curie

Marie Curie's life-story records a string of 'firsts'. She was the first woman to receive a PhD in France and the first woman to become a professor in a French university. Incredibly, not only was she the first woman to be awarded the Nobel Prize but she is the only person, man or woman, to have won it twice and for her work in two distinct areas of science. Here, then, is a life worthy of celebration.

It began in Poland in November 1867, where she first saw the light of day as Maria Salomea Sklodowska, growing up in Warsaw, which was then under Russian occupation. Her parents, both impoverished academics, were fiercely patriotic and their daughter received her tertiary education at the so-called 'Flying University', an underground educational establishment which aimed to provide a Polish education for its students, men and women, rather than have them indoctrinated with Russian principles of education. Though Marie never forgot her Polish heritage, she was not destined to remain in Poland.

Her older sister had married and settled in Paris and in 1891 Marie followed her, enrolling in the University of Paris in that same year. Subsidising her studies with some private teaching, she diligently pursued courses in physics, chemistry and mathematics but life was not easy. She had almost no money and often went without food in order to pay her way, but she achieved a degree in physics and met the man who was to change her life and her name.

Pierre Curie was an instructor at the School of Physics and Chemistry and, when he heard that Marie was looking for some laboratory space in which to conduct her research, he was pleased to help her. There developed between them not only a romance but also a close collaboration which would change the face of science and medicine, because Pierre was so intrigued by his wife's research projects that he gave up his own job to join her. They worked together in a leaky shed next to the School of Physics and Chemistry and in 1898 they published their discovery of two new elements, 'polonium' (which they are said to have named in honour of Marie's native Poland) and 'radium'. They coined the term 'radioactivity' and went on to investigate its potential benefits.

Soon, they began to be recognised for their ground-breaking work, though Marie had an uphill struggle to gain that recognition in the face of narrow-minded gender discrimination. The members of the Nobel committee, all males, refused to acknowledge that a woman could have undertaken this research and when the Curies were invited to address the Royal Institution in London, Marie, as a woman, was not allowed to speak. Eventually, the world began to recognise the sheer brilliance of their work and when, in 1906, Pierre was involved in a fatal road accident, his widow took over his teaching and carried on alone with their research.

Marie made no money from her discoveries; rather, she shared her knowledge and even took her expertise to the front in WWI, driving mobile x-ray vehicles and instructing others in using the on-board equipment to diagnose and treat injuries to French soldiers. Her eldest daughter, Iréne, carried on her mother's work, later earning another of the five Nobel prizes which were awarded in total to the members of the Curie family. But the dangerous nature of Marie's work with radioactivity had taken its toll and she died from the effects of excessive exposure to radiation. However, her legacy lives on in the UK charity which bears her name. There are several Marie Curie hospices, and the organisation also offers nursing care, helper services, information and support to individuals and their families living with a terminal illness.

ROSE
'NATASHA RICHARDSON'

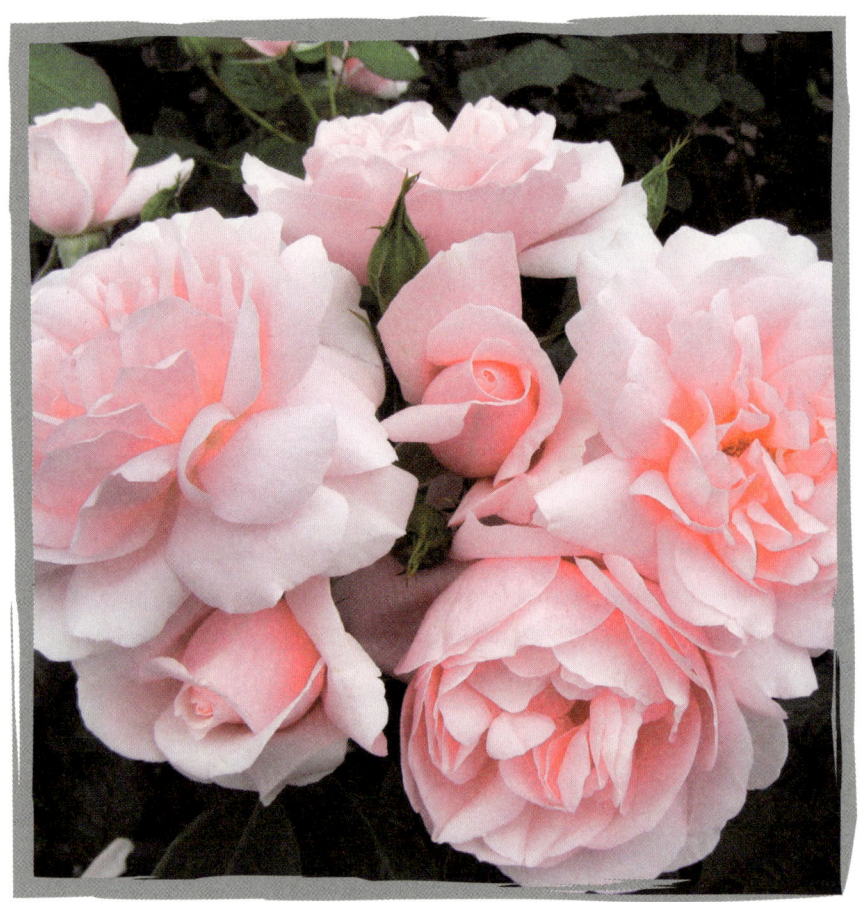

© Harkness Roses

Natasha Richardson

1963-2009

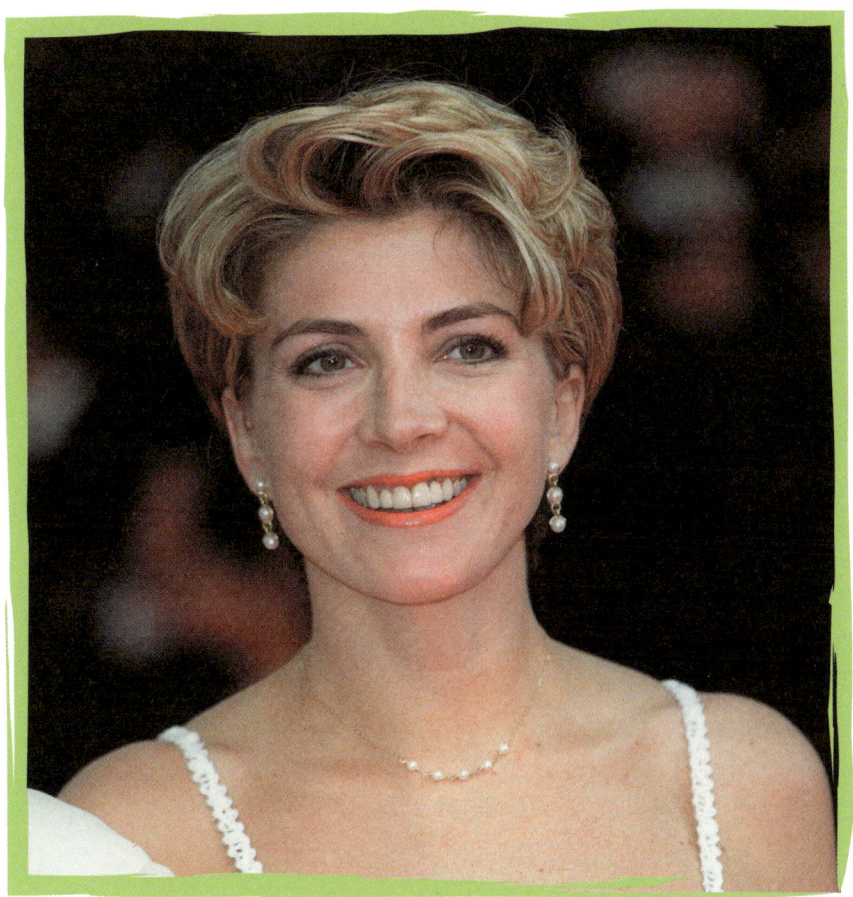

First nights? Film premieres? They were nothing unusual for
Natasha Richardson.

ROSE
'NATASHA RICHARDSON'
IN YOUR GARDEN

This delightful commemorative rose was launched at the Chelsea Flower Show in 2011. Like its namesake, the rose itself combines both charm and beauty and is the perfect blend of old and new. The blooms are reminiscent of Old English roses, with an enchanting perfume. Yet this is a modern rose, with incredible disease resistance, dense foliage and an abundance of pink flowers, which are pure and sharp in colour and plentiful in quantity. The bare root version can be planted up in beds, borders or hedges and makes a delightful cut flower for the vase.

It is also available as a half-standard rose which is grafted on to an 80cm (2ft 7in) stem and will grow yet further on that stem to make a 'flowering head', achieving a possible total height in excess of 1.4m (4.5ft). This provides an easy, satisfying way of adding height to the garden and, very often, half-standards are a better choice than full-standards in the average-sized garden, as they do not get too tall. The rose can also be provided as a pot-grown plant by arrangement with the nursery.

Harkness Roses, Cambridge Road, Hitchin, Herts, SG4 0JT.
Tel: 01462 420402. Email: harkness@roses.co.uk. www.roses.co.uk.
See also: The Rose Society UK. www.therosesociety.org.uk.

Natasha Richardson

You have only to mention the surname 'Redgrave' to a film fan or a theatre-goer and they'll know that you're talking about an actor. This distinguished acting dynasty, with its roots way back in the silent film era of the early 20th century, is now in its fifth generation. The family came to major prominence during the 1930s with Sir Michael Redgrave and his wife, Rachel Kempson, who established the family name firmly in the theatrical firmament. Their three children, Vanessa, Corin and Lynn, all continued the family tradition by also becoming distinguished actors.

Vanessa Redgrave married film-maker Tony Richardson in 1962 and the two daughters of the marriage, Natasha and Joely, went on to become... yes, of course, actors. But it was to Natasha's great credit that when, at the age of 17, she auditioned for a place at London's Central School of Speech and Drama, she did not disclose her family background; she wanted to be judged on her own merits. The fact that she was successful in her audition rather proves the point that she was, in any case, destined for the stage, and it was on the stage of the West Yorkshire Playhouse in Leeds that she made her professional acting debut.

Film and television roles soon followed, though she continued to work in the theatre. In 1985 she appeared to great acclaim alongside her mother, Vanessa, and her aunt, Lynn, as members of the same family in Chekov's *Three Sisters*. It was a memorable year for Natasha because her role in another Chekov play, *The Seagull*, won her the 'Plays and Players' most promising newcomer award for that year.

Now her film career began in earnest and she had starring roles in several notable films. In 1990, she won the first of her two *Evening Standard* British Film Awards for Best Actress in *The Handmaid's Tale* and *The Comfort of Strangers*. In the same year, she married her first husband, film-maker Robert Fox, though the marriage was not destined to last, possibly not helped by the fact that Natasha was now in great demand on both sides of the Atlantic. She starred on Broadway in the Eugene O'Neill play *Anna Christie* and, two years later, she married the man who had been her co-star in that production, the Irish-born actor Liam Neeson. Natasha loved New York, as did her new husband, and they were both very successful there. Natasha won a Tony award in the role of Sally Bowles in *Cabaret* and Neeson was nominated 'Best Actor' for his starring role in the film *Schindler's List*. Husband and wife both took American citizenship and, with a good marriage and two young sons, the world was at their feet. Theirs was a show business success story; sadly, it did not have a happy ending.

On a skiing holiday in 2009, Natasha, a novice on the slopes, fell and sustained a serious head injury. Despite being airlifted to a

New York hospital for emergency treatment, she died two days later on 18th March, leaving her young family devastated by her premature death at the age of forty-five.

Despite her busy acting career, Natasha found time to work tirelessly for charity. She had been deeply affected, at the age of eleven, to learn of her father's bisexuality, and Tony Richardson died from AIDS-related causes in 1991. Thereafter, Natasha helped to raise millions of dollars in the fight against the disease. An ambassador for the National AIDS Trust, she also received the Award of Courage of the American Foundation for AIDS Research (amfAR), becoming a board member of the organisation in 2006.

This fine actress leaves an enduring reputation, clearly well-qualified to take her rightful place in the Redgrave dynasty. And on 19th March 2009, the lights of every theatre on Broadway in New York and in London's West End were dimmed, to mark the eclipse of one of the acting profession's brightest stars.

CHRYSANTHEMUM
'NELL GWYNN'

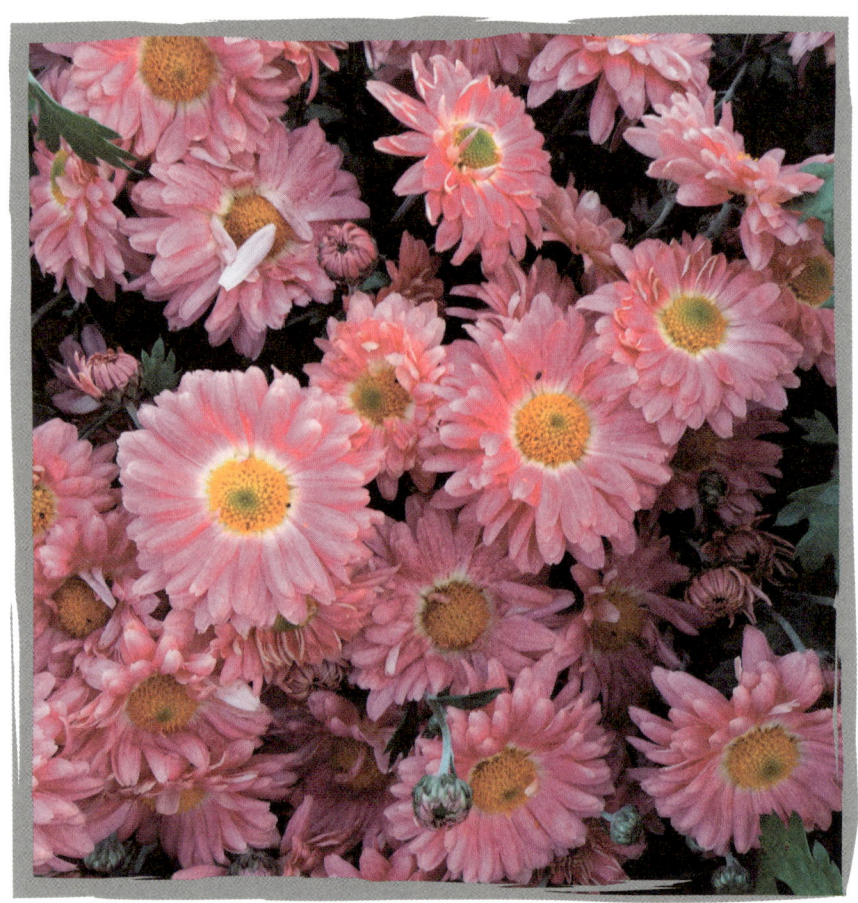

© Halls of Heddon

Nell Gwynn

1650-1687

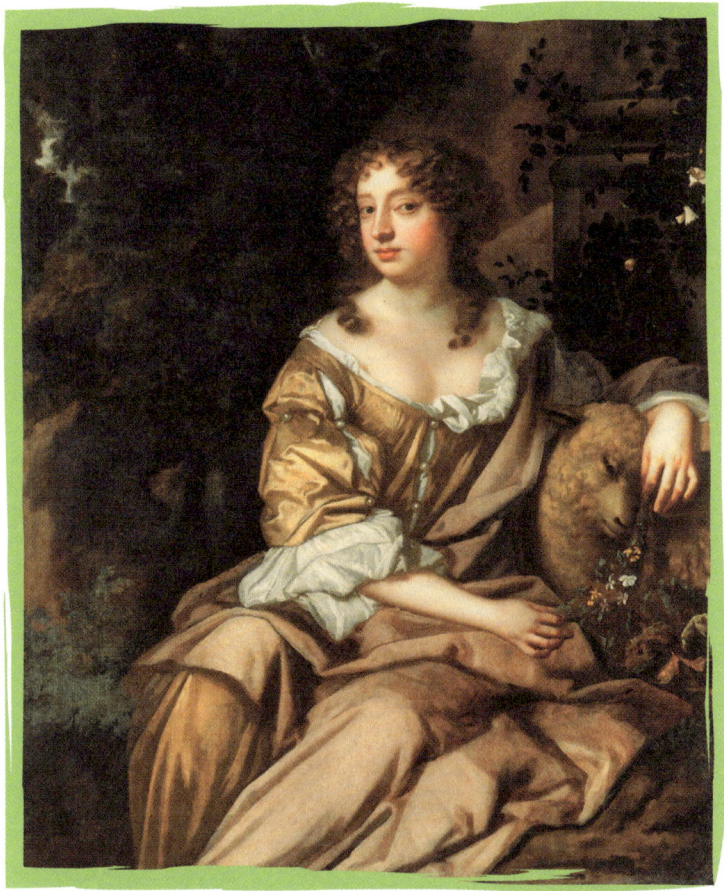

The 'rags to riches' story was never more true than it was for
'pretty, witty' Nell Gwynn.

CHRYSANTHEMUM
'NELL GWYNN'
IN YOUR GARDEN

This hardy chrysanthemum produces attractive double pink flowers and is wonderfully versatile. The chrysanthemum's ability to last well in the vase has made it a valuable commercial crop and it really is the darling of the florists' shop but it is always worth remembering its value in the garden.

Growing to a height of 45cm (17.5in), it is thoroughly reliable, flowering relatively late in the summer but continuing to flower right through to winter.

Competitive gardeners will be more than familiar with the sight of the show benches at autumn shows filled with the astounding and much-admired colourful blooms and sprays of chrysanthemums.

Halls of Heddon produces a brief guide to growing chrysanthemums, available through the website, and the National Chrysanthemum Society, too, has produced some helpful publications which will enable the first-time grower to get the very best from their plants.

Halls of Heddon, West Heddon Nursery Centre,
Heddon-on-the-Wall, Newcastle-upon-Tyne, NE15 0JS.
Tel: 01661 852 445. Email: enquiry@hallsofheddon.co.uk.
www.hallsofheddon.com. See also: The National Chrysanthemum Society. www.nationalchrysanthemumsociety.co.uk.

Nell Gwynn

Charming, clever, playful; these are all adjectives which can be used to describe King Charles II's most famous mistress, but she was also both shrewd and astute. She needed to be: Eleanor Gwynn, always known as 'Nell', was a woman who lived by her wits.

Nell's background was one of extreme poverty, though details of her birth were unrecorded and the spelling of her surname varies. The city of Hereford lays claim to have been her birthplace, and to this day one of its streets is named 'Gwynne Street' in support of this, but equally, she might have been born in Oxford or in London's Covent Garden. Her exact parentage, too, is difficult to ascertain. Her father is likely to have been a Captain Thomas Gwynn who claimed descent from 'an ancient family in Wales' and, indeed, the surname is a Welsh one, meaning 'white'. But it's unlikely that Nell's father had married her mother, who was a 'madam', the keeper of a brothel which might have been in Covent Garden or in Coal Yard Alley, a poor slum near Drury Lane. It's also possible that Nell might have worked there as a child prostitute. One of the few certainties is that her degenerate mother met her death by drowning in a ditch near Westminster while drunk. It was hardly an auspicious start in life for Nell, a girl who harboured theatrical ambitions.

In the seventeenth century, the words 'actress' and 'prostitute' were synonymous. It had only been a short time since women were allowed to appear on stage and this was at the behest of the popular King Charles II, who took his place on the throne in 1660 and was known with affection as the 'Merry Monarch'. After the strict Puritan deprivations of the Cromwellian era, Charles lost little time in licensing two of London's theatres, with the proviso that female roles be played by 'their natural performers', i.e. women. Until then, all the great female roles in theatre, including Shakespeare's 'Juliet', 'Lady Macbeth' and others, had been played by young boys. But it was some time before women came to be taken seriously as actresses. Nell's first experience of theatre was as one of a group of young women who were employed to sell sweetmeats and fruit to the audience, including the small, so-called 'china' oranges for a few pence each. They would also often convey messages from the men in the audience to the actresses backstage to arrange assignations of a dubious nature.

But there was more to Nell than this. Within a year she was appearing on stage, playing opposite her real-life lover, the actor Charles Hart. At first, she wasn't very impressive, only finding her métier a year or so later in the bawdy 'Restoration' comedies of such writers as John Dryden. Her comedy acting was, by all accounts, superb, and Samuel Pepys, a regular theatre-goer, called her 'pretty, witty Nell'. She had also taken a second lover called Charles: he was Charles Sackville, Lord Buckhurst, and with him, young Nell began to move in aristocratic circles. Then, in 1668, when King Charles II became her lover, he is said to have found it amusing that she referred to him in private as 'Charles the Third'! Of course, the King was married but hadn't fathered any children by his wife, Catherine of Braganza. On the other hand, he had about a dozen children by various mistresses and acknowledged them all by granting them aristocratic titles. In fact, the descendants of some are still among the English aristocracy to this day. But when he still hadn't ennobled young Charles, his first child by Nell and whom she had named after the King, she took matters into her own hands. She is said to have summoned the six-year-old to her in the King's presence by saying: 'Come here, you little bastard, and say hello to your father!' The King immediately created him Earl of Burford.

'Pretty, witty Nell' remained a royal favourite and did well out of her relationship with the King. He provided generously for her with money and property, and even on his deathbed he entreated his brother James, who succeeded him, to 'let not poor Nelly starve.' James honoured her debts and on her own death three years later, she left a legacy in her will to the prisoners of Newgate.

NASTURTIUM
'PEACH MELBA'

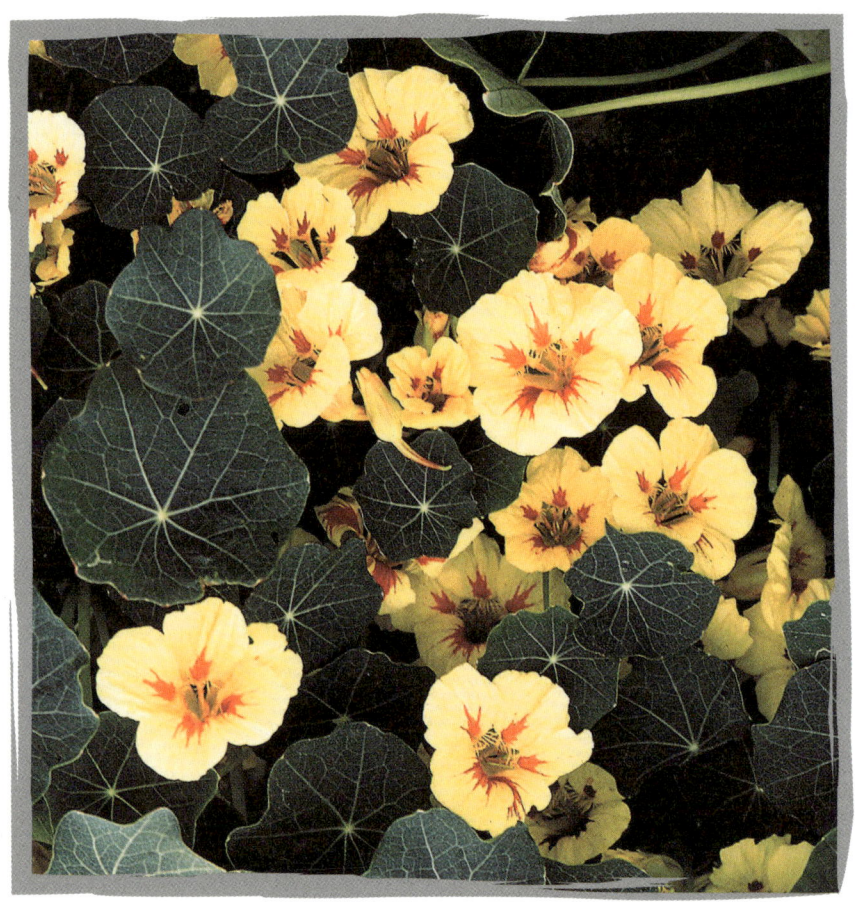

© Thompson & Morgan

Nellie Melba

1861-1931

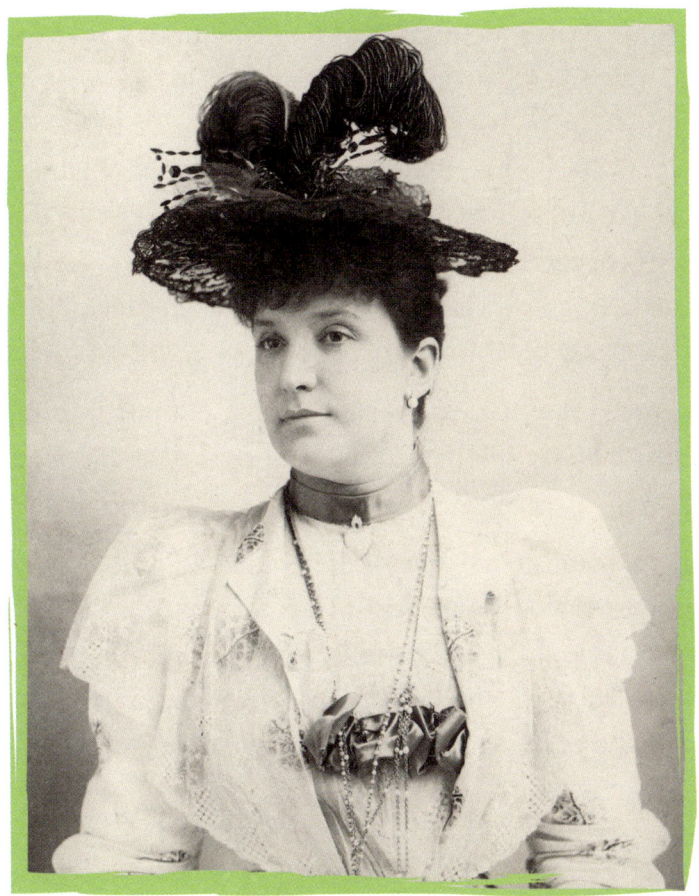

The voice of Nellie Melba was an inspiration for composers,
audiences... and chefs!

NASTURTIUM
'PEACH MELBA'
IN YOUR GARDEN

Nasturtium 'Peach Melba' (*Tropaeolum majus*) is a pretty variety with a lovely free-flowering habit. Seed should be sown outdoors in a sunny spot, in drills spaced 30cm (12in) apart where they are to grow. This is best done from March to May. Seed should be covered with its own depth of well-drained, well-raked soil. Seedlings appear after 7-12 days and they should be thinned out to 30cm (12in) apart when they're large enough to handle. Water regularly, especially during dry periods.

This easy-to-grow, hardy annual produces a fabulous display of creamy blooms, splashed with burnt-orange at the centre of each flower.

True to its name, it looks good enough to eat – and it really is! The peppery flavour of the leaves and colourful flowers will enrich salads and the unripe seeds can be used like capers; delicious combined with cream cheese or butter in canapés. And pollinating insects love these pretty nasturtium flowers too!

Thompson & Morgan Ltd, Poplar Lane, Ipswich, IP8 3BU.
Tel: 0844 573 1818. www.thompson-morgan.com.
See also: RHS advice. www.rhs.org.uk/Plants.

Nellie Melba

It's not often that you would associate an operatic soprano with a dish of peaches in raspberry sauce, or with thinly-sliced toast. But the very fact that the great French chef Auguste Escoffier named no less than four of his signature dishes after Dame Nellie Melba is an indication of her enormous popularity at the turn of the twentieth century.

Helen ('Nellie') Porter Mitchell was born in Melbourne, Australia, just nine years after her father had emigrated there from his native Scotland. He had quickly established himself as a successful builder, enabling him to give his daughter an excellent education that included piano and singing lessons. Naturally gifted, Nellie proved to be adept musically and sang frequently in amateur concerts, as well as playing the organ in church. She continued to study singing but, perhaps because her father disapproved of any suggestion that she might make it a career, she made a disastrous marriage at the age of twenty-one which ended in a bitter separation barely a year later. Now she really was determined to sing for a living and achieved a good deal of early success in her home country. Building on that, she decided to try her luck in London but she didn't impress the English entrepreneurs of the time, people like Sir Arthur Sullivan and Carl Rosa. Undeterred, she travelled to Paris and here she found a teacher who recognised her star quality and nurtured it. It was after she had been offered a lucrative contract to sing at the Théâtre de la Monnaie in Brussels that she adopted the stage name of 'Melba' from Melbourne, her home city. She never looked back.

It took Melba some time to make her mark in London and it was only thanks to the support and encouragement of her friend Lady Constance Lonsdale, wife of the 4th Earl of Lonsdale and a famous patron of the arts, that she appeared at Covent Garden in 1889. Here she met with great success before returning to Paris. Though her Australian accent was ill-suited to singing in French, the French composer Léo Delibes said it didn't matter if she sang in Chinese – as long as she sang!

Melba's love affair with the Duke of Orléans in the early 1890s was the subject of much gossip and great controversy but it provided Melba's husband with the excuse to divorce her and she never re-married. Rather, the pattern was set for the future and it consisted of appearances at all the great opera houses of Europe and New York as well as frequent touring of Australia and New Zealand, which gave her an impressive income. Melba was a singer blessed with a pure, lyrical soprano voice and sparklingly clear coloratura techniques, so she never attempted to sing the heavier German repertoire. Rather, her preference was for the works of Puccini, Verdi and the Italian school and she famously appeared opposite the internationally famous tenor Enrico Caruso in many memorable performances. American audiences loved her, too, and the *New York Times* declared that she had 'one of the loveliest voices that ever issued from a human throat'.

Melba returned to Australia in 1909 and was instrumental in setting up what later became the Melbourne Conservatory of Music. Then, when war broke out in 1914, she set about organising concerts which would raise a total of more than £100,000 for war charities, a phenomenal amount at that time. In recognition of this, she was made a Dame Commander of the Order of the British Empire in 1918, elevated to Dame Grand Cross of the Order in 1927.

After her death in 1931, it was a measure of her fame and popularity that her funeral cavalcade was over a kilometre long. Memorials to her include several busts and statues as well as a stained glass window in the London church of St. Sepulchre, popularly known as 'the musicians' church'. Her image appears on an Australian $100 dollar note. Dame Nellie Melba lies buried in Scots' Church, Melbourne, which was built by her father and where she, as a young girl, had sung in the choir.

AQUILEGIA
'NORA BARLOW'

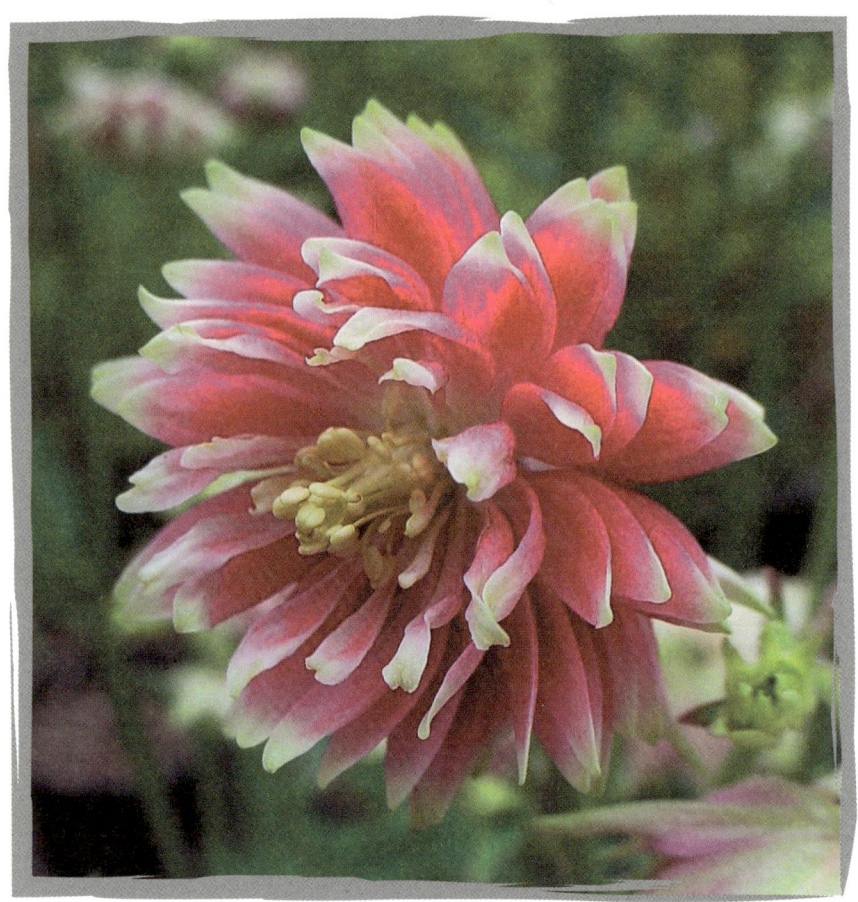

© Parker's Dutch Bulbs Ltd.

Nora Barlow

1885-1989

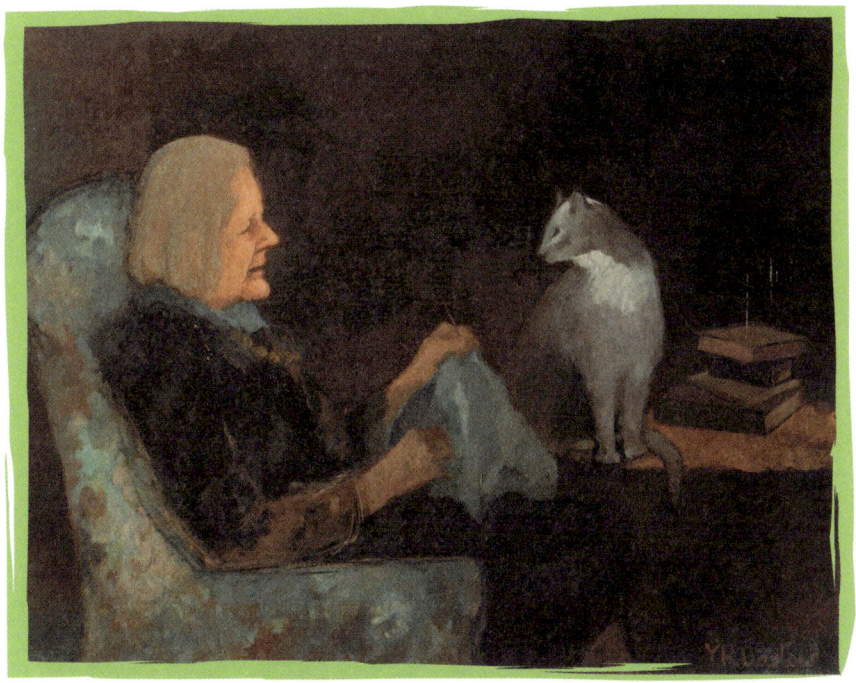

Nora, Lady Barlow, towards the end of her long life. In this informal painting by her daughter-in-law Yvonne Barlow, she shares an affectionate moment with her cat, Chico.

AQUILEGIA
'NORA BARLOW'
IN YOUR GARDEN

Aquilegia vulgaris is also known as the 'Columbine Plant' or, most charmingly, 'Granny's Bonnet' and is a much-loved, familiar perennial in the cottage garden.

Aquilegia 'Nora Barlow' is one of the most attractive varieties, bearing almost spherical, full double flower heads with masses of pink, white-tipped petals encircling golden yellow sepals, set against a background of lush, ferny foliage.

It is grown for its graceful, upright habit, reaching a height of around 60cm (23in) and a spread of 30cm (12in). Given any sunny or partly-shaded place in a moist but well-drained soil, it rewards the gardener with perpetual flowers from May to July, especially if these are regularly dead-headed.

Fully hardy, it benefits from being carefully lifted and divided every three to five years and an annual mulch with well-rotted manure or compost will pay dividends. Aquilegias are prone to self-seeding around the garden and bees simply can't resist them.

J. Parker's Dutch Bulbs Ltd, 14 Hadfield Street, Old Trafford, Manchester, M16 9FG. Tel: 0161 848 1100. Email: sales@jparkers.co.uk. www.jparkers.co.uk. See also: RHS advice. www.rhs.org.uk/Plants.

Nora Barlow

Emma Nora Darwin's maiden name gives us the first clue to her identity – she was the granddaughter of Charles Darwin (1809-1882), the British scientist who first propounded the theory on the process of evolution and did more to influence the way we now think about the natural world than anyone else, before or since. Her father, Sir Horace Darwin (1851-1928) was a civil engineer who founded the Cambridge Scientific Instrument Company.

Nora had a lot to live up to but nothing daunted her and, probably with enormous encouragement from her scientifically-minded family, she took up the study of Botany at Cambridge, becoming a student of William Bateson's course on 'variation and heredity' in 1906. Bateson taught the theories of Mendelism, based on the work of Gregor Johann Mendel, a nineteenth-century Austrian priest-scientist who had experimented widely in the field of plant hybridisation. Nora's interest in the subject was stimulated, perhaps, by the fact that her grandfather, though he had caused such a stir with his theory of the mechanics of evolution, had been barking up slightly the wrong tree when it came to heredity. Darwin had been quite unaware of the ground-breaking work which Mendel was doing in Moravia (the eastern part of today's Czech Republic) – though that is hardly surprising since Mendel's theories were widely discounted until after his death in 1884, two years after Darwin himself had died. The nineteenth century was a time of great scientific discoveries, from evolution and photoconductivity to germ theory, thermodynamics and a great deal more besides. Those were exciting times but scientific thinking and methodology did much to upend the religious dogma which had gone unquestioned hitherto and this led to tensions between religious and scientific communities.

In 1911, Nora married Alan Barlow, the son of the royal physician who had attended Queen Victoria. During the next decade, Nora gave birth to six children but managed to continue studying 'genetics', as the new science had been named by her former tutor, William Bateson. In 1910, Bateson had been made Director of the newly-established John Innes Horticultural Institute, the first UK centre for research in plant breeding and genetics. Somehow, Nora, now entirely fascinated by this new science, found time to work there each summer. Appropriately, her work at the Institute centred on aquilegias and, in an attempt to divert her children, she had shown them how to break off an aquilegia's spur and suck out the nectar. Her granddaughter, the poet Ruth Padel, remembers her own mother, Nora's daughter Hilda, describing the technique and recalling that Nora protected the plants she was working on by tying little muslin bags over their heads, rather than risk having her research ruined by her children's enthusiastic attentions. An article on Ruth Padel's own website recalls her grandmother in fascinating detail (see Further Information on page 201).

Nora lived to be 103 years old and her great-niece, the historical novelist Emma Darwin, has a childhood memory of her at the age of ninety but, Emma says, still 'sharp as a tack', presiding over a big family party in honour of her birthday. Somehow, the cake actually accommodated ninety candles but they generated so much heat that they started to bend and had to be treated as a fire hazard.

During the course of this long and enormously rewarding life, Nora edited and published a total of five books, including Charles Darwin's full and unexpurgated autobiography, which had previously had personal and religious material removed from it. She also edited many of her grandfather's notes as well as his correspondence with his tutor and mentor, John Stevens Henslow.

It must have been a great source of pleasure and pride for Nora that, during her lifetime, the accepted view of evolution came to combine Mendelian genetics with her own grandfather's theory of natural selection.

PELARGONIUM
'OCTAVIA HILL'

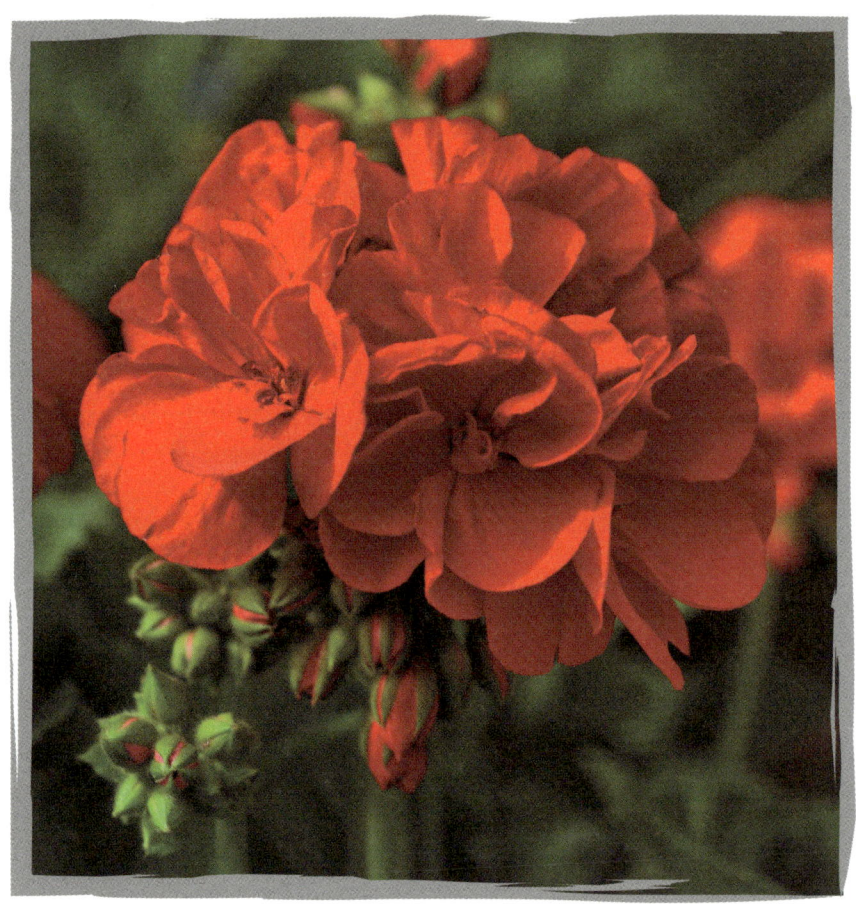

© Thompson & Morgan

Octavia Hill

1838–1912

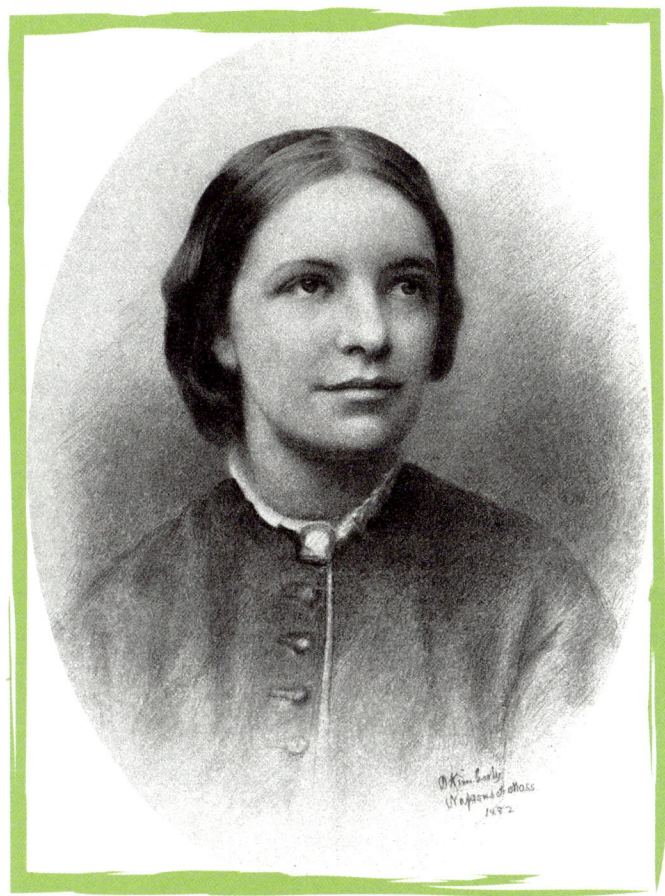

Londoners should never take a walk on Hampstead Heath
without remembering the debt they owe Octavia Hill.

PELARGONIUM 'OCTAVIA HILL'

IN YOUR GARDEN

Enormous heads of scarlet blooms with exceptional weather resistance mean that this stunning pelargonium stands out dramatically in a patio display or when filling the gaps in a border. If it is deadheaded regularly, the plant will reward the attentive gardener with abundant flowers and vigorous growth throughout the summer, reaching a height of 50cm (20in) and a spread of 45cm (18in). And if the growing tip of each stem is pinched out, this will also encourage branching to form a bushier plant.

Pelargoniums are often popularly called 'geraniums' but this is not correct. True geraniums are hardy. Pelargoniums are not. Pelargoniums are really only half hardy but, with care, they may be potted up and overwintered in a frost free greenhouse. In spring, when all risk of frost has passed, they should be gradually acclimatised to outdoor conditions over a period of seven to ten days before transplanting them into their final positions in containers, beds and borders. They prefer a sunny or semi-shaded position in any light, non-acidic, well-drained soil.

Thompson & Morgan Ltd, Poplar Lane, Ipswich, IP8 3BU.
Tel: 0844 573 1818. www.thompson-morgan.com.
See also: The Pelargonium & Geranium Society. www.thepags.org.uk.

Octavia Hill

Octavia Hill is chiefly remembered as one of the founders of The National Trust – but there was a lot more to her than that. An indefatigable social reformer, she found inspiration in a line from a poem by Charles Kingsley in which he advised: 'Do noble things, not dream them, all day long' and she spent a lifetime in following his advice, particularly when it came to improving the living conditions and built environment of the poorest in society.

Around the time of Octavia's birth, her parents, James and Caroline Hill, had opened a school for infants in Wisbech as 'a service to the wretched poor'. They were passionate reformers and admirers of Robert Owen's philanthropic ideals. They could well afford to make such a grand gesture; James Hill was a wealthy man, a successful corn merchant, despite having lost money in the banking crisis of 1825. Later, however, he suffered a nervous breakdown from which he never recovered.

Caroline Southwood Hill, Octavia's mother, was a writer and educationist, and when she was forced by her husband's illness to assume responsibility for the welfare of the whole family, she turned to her own father, Dr. Thomas Southwood Smith, for help. Southwood Smith was a physician to the London Fever Hospital and a health reformer who campaigned tirelessly on social issues. He asserted, rightly, that the absence of drainage in the homes of the poor was the major cause of cholera, which claimed 126 lives every day in England.

Southwood Smith's house in North London became a second home to the Hill family and under his influence his daughter and young granddaughter, Octavia, learned the reasons for his strongly held views on the need for government reform in providing housing for the poor. They shared their views with the like-minded members of London's Christian Socialist circle, among them John Ruskin, who wanted to bring about change.

Ruskin was a very influential man who, as well as being a social thinker and, later, a philanthropist, was a celebrated artist and art critic. A talented painter in her own right, Octavia then trained with Ruskin and her first employment was as an art copyist. And Octavia needed to earn: she and her sisters were constantly under pressure to repay their father's debts.

Ruskin's own father died in 1864, leaving his substantial fortune to his only son, who promptly began to spend it by investing in Octavia's dream of establishing social housing for the poor of London. This she arranged to have cleared, cleaned, repaired and redecorated. As their 'landlady', Octavia paid these properties weekly visits, not only to collect the rents but to persuade the women who lived there to take a pride in themselves, their families and their homes. She also encouraged their awareness of gardens and parks. The tenants responded very positively, appreciating the fact that someone was taking an interest in them and their welfare. As Ruskin financed the purchase of yet more properties for her scheme, so other investors became interested in the work and, by 1874, Octavia and her fellow workers controlled over 3,000 tenancies on seventeen sites around London. She wrote and published articles on her work and, as the system gathered momentum, so it created interest and admiration from all over the country and abroad.

This, then, was Octavia Hill's life's work. She was a celebrated social reformer and, crucially, she also realised the benefits of parks and open spaces in towns where overcrowding and poor housing conditions had been allowed to proliferate. This was what inspired her successful campaign to save London's Hampstead Heath and Parliament Hill Fields from housing developers. Then, in 1895, she became one of the three founders of the National Trust, a charity set up to preserve buildings of historic interest and areas of natural beauty for the enjoyment of everyone. The effects of her dedication, her determination and vision continue to benefit our quality of life to this day. We owe Octavia Hill an enormous debt of gratitude.

PRIMULA AURICULA
'ODETTE'

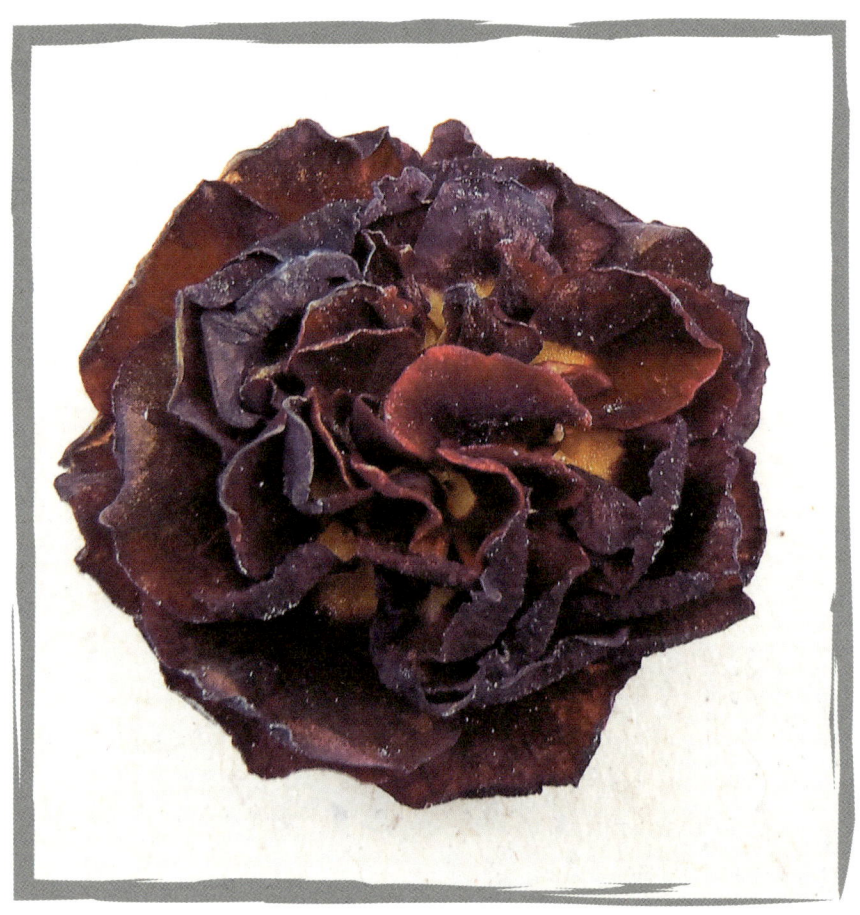

© Hillview Hardy Plants Ltd

Odette

1912–1995

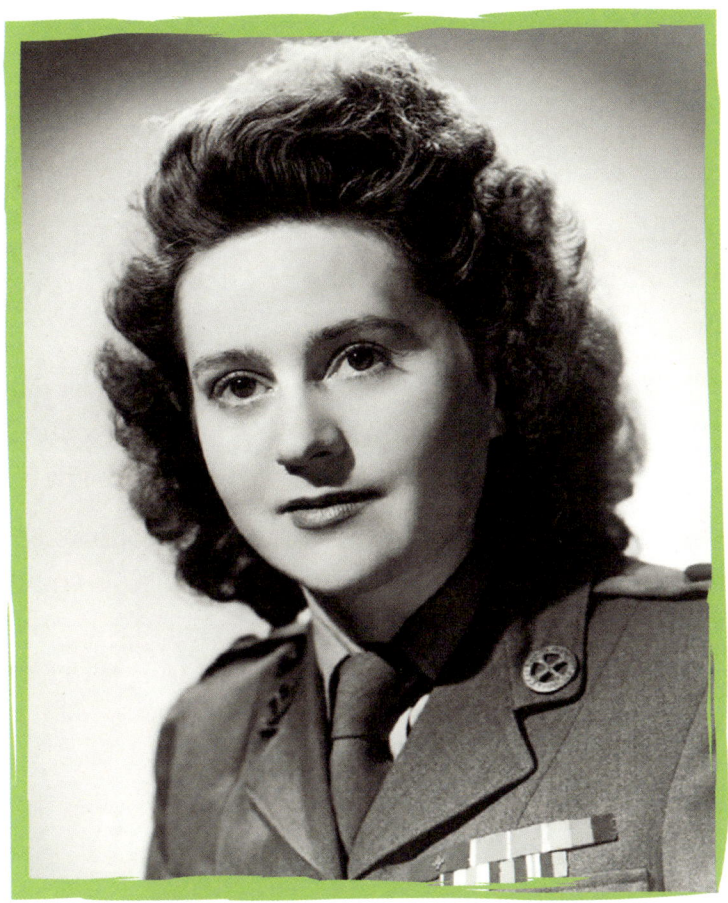

Odette's love of her native France and her 'adopted' country of
England led her into the defence of both.

PRIMULA AURICULA
'ODETTE'
IN YOUR GARDEN

Alpine and border auriculas are easily grown outside but their preference is for cool conditions; cold is never a problem for any auricula. They're fairly dormant during the winter, closing themselves down until they start back into growth in the spring.

Then they appreciate plenty of light but not the full sun of summer, it's probably best to compromise and plant them in a partially shaded area of the garden.

They do well in humus-rich soil and appreciate being watered – but not too much. It's wise to divide the plants in the summer if they get too big or are not flowering as well as they might be.

They are prone to attack by vine weevils and root aphids, so keep an eye open for those unwelcome pests. Auriculas thrive if the soil is improved with a slow-release fertiliser and they appreciate a top-up feed of tomato fertiliser during the growing season.

Hillview Hardy Plants Ltd, Worfield, Bridgnorth,
Shropshire, WV15 5NT. Tel: 01746 716 454. Email: hillview@onetel.net.
www.hillviewhardyplants.com. See also: The National Auricula &
Primula Society UK. www.auriculaandprimula.org.uk.

Odette

This courageous woman does not need to be identified by her full name but the register of births at Amiens in northern France records that Odette Marie Céline Brailly was born there in 1912 to a banker and his wife. Six years later, Odette had lost her father, who was killed in the Battle of Verdun during the First World War, and it was for service in the Second World War that his daughter became the first woman ever to be awarded the George Cross for outstanding bravery.

In 1931, Odette married an Englishman named Roy Patrick Sansom and the couple moved from France to England in 1933. They had three daughters but, once again, Odette's peaceful family life was disrupted by war when her husband was called up for active service. Odette settled with the children in Somerset, where she happened to hear a radio appeal for any photographs of France that might help the war effort. She collated the holiday snaps of her childhood and duly posted them off to the War Office, where they created such interest that she was invited to explain their detailed locations. At that interview the suggestion was made that she, as a fluent French-speaker, could help the war effort immeasurably by joining the Special Operations Executive (the SOE), based in France. So, with her daughters safely in the care of a nearby convent school, she was given training and kitted out with French clothes, French shoes, forged French identity papers and even French-style fillings in her teeth! With the code-name 'Lise' and under cover as a member of the First Aid Nursing Yeomanry, Odette made the crossing to occupied France to join the resistance group in Auxerre.

Here she worked alongside a colleague named Peter Morland Churchill and, after the Nazis had invaded in 1942, she carried on working as his courier. The following April, they were both betrayed by a double agent and arrested by the Germans. Under intensely harsh questioning by the Gestapo while being subjected to extremely painful torture techniques, Odette remained silent except that she managed to convince the Nazis that Peter Churchill was related to the British Prime Minister Winston Churchill – which he wasn't. She was condemned to death on two separate counts, accused of being a British spy and, as a French woman, found guilty of crimes under German law. Her response to these accusations was: 'you must take your pick, gentlemen. I can only die once.' Shortly afterwards, she was moved to the women's concentration camp at Ravensbrück, near Berlin. Here she was kept in solitary confinement near the punishment block, where the miseries of her incarceration and torture were heightened by the sounds of beatings, executions and the rumble of carts taking the previous night's dead to the crematorium. She was kept alive only because her captors were still unsure about the possible connection with Winston

Churchill. The privations of her imprisonment took their toll and it was while Odette was in the camp hospital suffering from tuberculosis in 1945 that the war came to an end and she was finally released. Subsequently, she gave evidence against the Nazis at the Nüremberg trials and, on her return to England, she was made an MBE. Odette was awarded the George Cross in 1946. This is the UK's second-highest award for courage, given for acts of the greatest heroism or for the most conspicuous courage in circumstances of extreme danger. During the following year, 1947, after her divorce from her first husband, she and Peter Churchill were married.

A book about her life was published in 1949 and later made into a film in which the actress Anna Neagle gave a moving performance in the title role. The film ends with a statement from Odette in which she simply says:

'I am a very ordinary woman to whom a chance was given to see human beings at their best and at their worst. My colleagues, who did far more than I and suffered far more profoundly, are not here to speak. It is to their memory that this film has been made and I would like it to be a window through which may be seen those very gallant women with whom I had the honour to serve.'

CLEMATIS
'FAIR ROSAMUND'

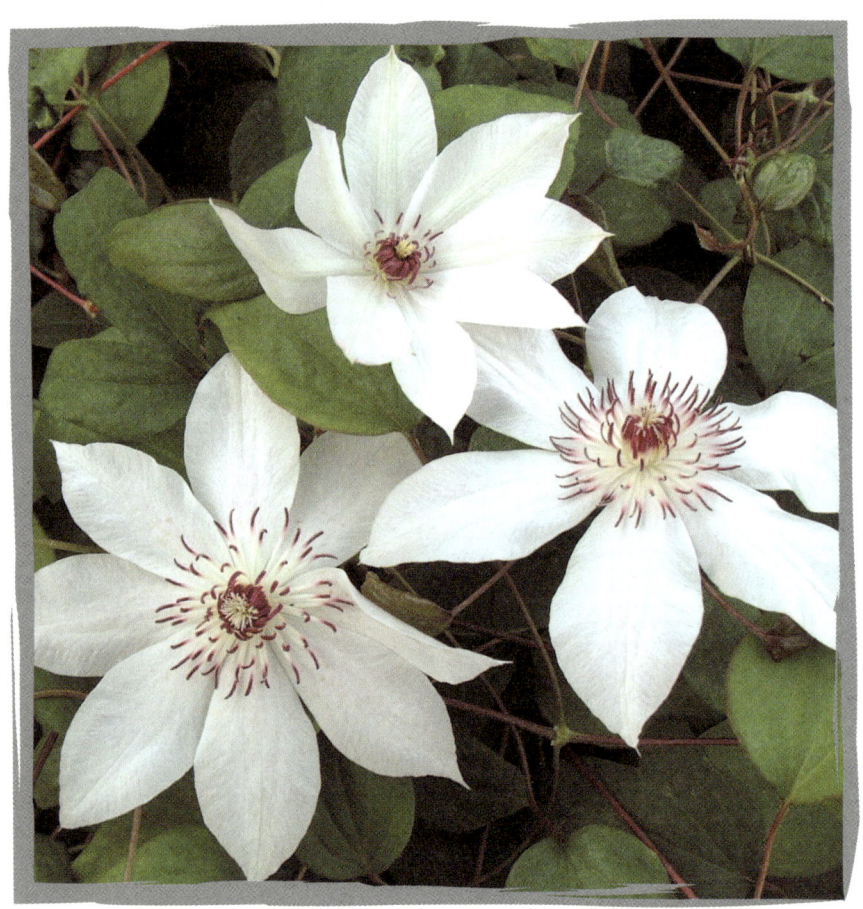

© Taylors Clematis

Rosamund Clifford

c1140-1175/6

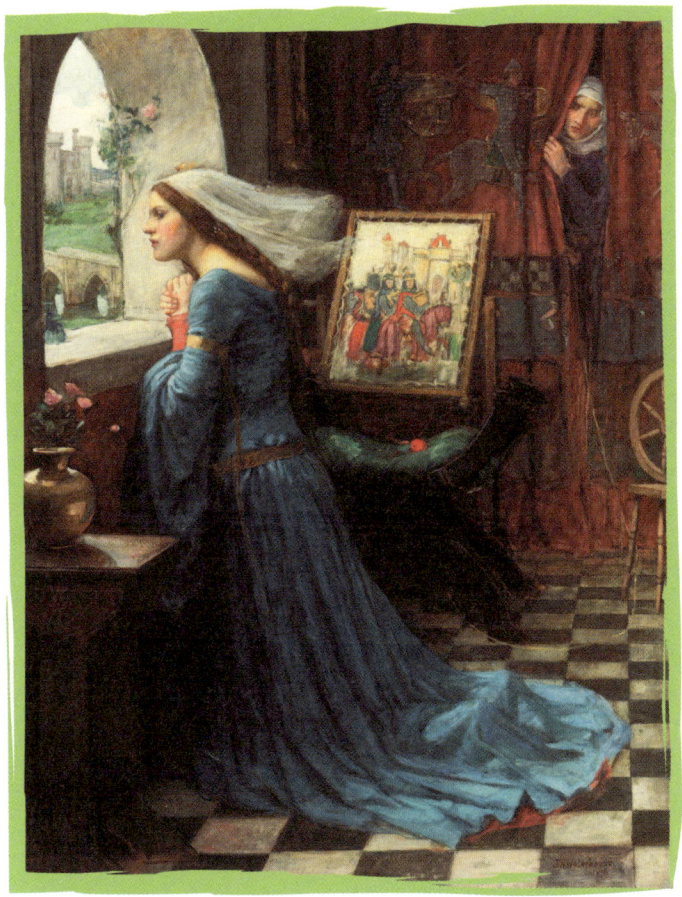

'Fair Rosamund' awaiting the arrival of her royal lover.
A painting by John William Waterhouse, 1916.

CLEMATIS
'FAIR ROSAMUND'
IN YOUR GARDEN

First grown by the Jackman nursery in 1871, the clematis 'Fair Rosamund' belongs to that second wave of large-flowered hybrids that come along fairly late in the spring, blooming on the year-old wood. 'Fair Rosamund' reliably produces two good flushes of bloom in a year.

Preferring sun or part shade, the young plant is of bushy habit and readily sends up new stems from the base. Ordinarily, it will reach roughly 2m-3m (6in-9in).

One word of warning – the stems are relatively thin and care should be taken if it becomes necessary to disentangle them. If the spring has been cold, the first flowers may have a ghostly midrib of green or grey but the blossoms that open soon afterwards will return to form with blush-white tepals soon fading to white, set off by that splendid boss in the centre. The scent is delicious.

Taylors Clematis, Sutton Road, Sutton, Doncaster, South Yorkshire, DN6 9JZ. Tel. 01302 700716. Email: info@taylorsclematis.co.uk. www.taylorsclematis.co.uk. See also: The British Clematis Society. www.britishclematis.org.uk.

Rosamund Clifford

If, some moonlit night, you were to walk beside the waters of the Thames at Godstow Lock to the north of Oxford, you should not be surprised to encounter the wraith-like figure of a young woman on the riverbank, pitifully mourning the loss of her love. At least that's the story that the good citizens of Oxford have been telling for more than eight hundred years.

The ghost is reputedly that of *Fair Rosamund*, whose name probably derives from the Latin *rosa mundi* – meaning the 'rose of the world'. Certainly, Rosamund Clifford was famed for her beauty, which, probably sometime around 1163, had won her the lustful attention of King Henry II. The King chose to ignore the inconvenient fact that he already had a wife, the single-minded, feisty, controversial Queen Eleanor of Aquitaine – and Eleanor was having none of his nonsense. Despite all that, Rosamund was said to have been the great love of Henry's life.

During the twelfth century, one of the royal family's favourite palaces was at Woodstock, near Oxford, occupying roughly the site where Blenheim Palace now stands, and a pool in the grounds of the palace is known to this day as 'Fair Rosamund's Well'. Legend has it that King Henry built a beautiful tower at Woodstock, surrounded by a maze, as a place to hide his fair Rosamund from the jealous, vindictive Queen Eleanor. But according to the fable, Eleanor, determined to get the better of her younger, more beautiful rival, went in search of her at Woodstock. Outside the maze, she found a silken thread which had become unravelled from Rosamund's embroidery and followed it until she found her hiding in the tower. A furious Eleanor stood over a cowering Rosamund, threatening her with death, but generously offered her the choice between a dagger and a cup of poison. Rosamund is said to have chosen the poison. There is probably absolutely no truth in the story but it is one of the many myths which have surrounded Fair Rosamund for centuries. One story tells of Queen Eleanor having her rival roasted between two fires, stabbed and left to bleed to death in a bath of scalding water. Story-tellers can be blood-thirsty individuals!

There is no evidence that Rosamund ever gave her royal lover any children, though there has been much conjecture that she might have done. Neither is it possible to say with any certainty whether she accompanied the King on his travels or whether he kept her in absolute seclusion at Woodstock. This has provided several historical novelists with the licence to paint some imagined detail onto her life. Among those who have featured her in novels about Henry and Eleanor are Sharon Penman, Norah Lofts, Jean Plaidy and Alison Weir.

The King's relationship with his lover seems to have become public knowledge sometime around 1174 and it is known that Rosamund, greatly embarrassed by the immodest reputation she had acquired as the King's mistress, wanted to bring the affair to a close. So, in 1176, she entered Godstow, the nunnery where she had received her own early education. She died there soon afterwards and King Henry, heartbroken, according to legend, commissioned an ornate tomb for her near the high altar in the Priory church.

But when the bishop of Lincoln visited Godstow in 1191, two years after the King's own death, he was appalled to find Rosamund's tomb laden with flowers and candles, quite clearly venerated. Disgusted that a paramour should be accorded such a privilege, the bishop ordered that the tomb be dismantled and Rosamund's remains re-interred outside the church. The ruins of Godstow Priory church still stand but, should you choose to visit them at night, be prepared to encounter the poor disturbed spirit of Rosamund Clifford, doomed to spend eternity in nocturnal wanderings and outpourings of ghostly grief on the riverbank, bemoaning her lost love and searching in vain for a final resting place.

HERBACEOUS PEONY 'SARAH BERNHARDT'

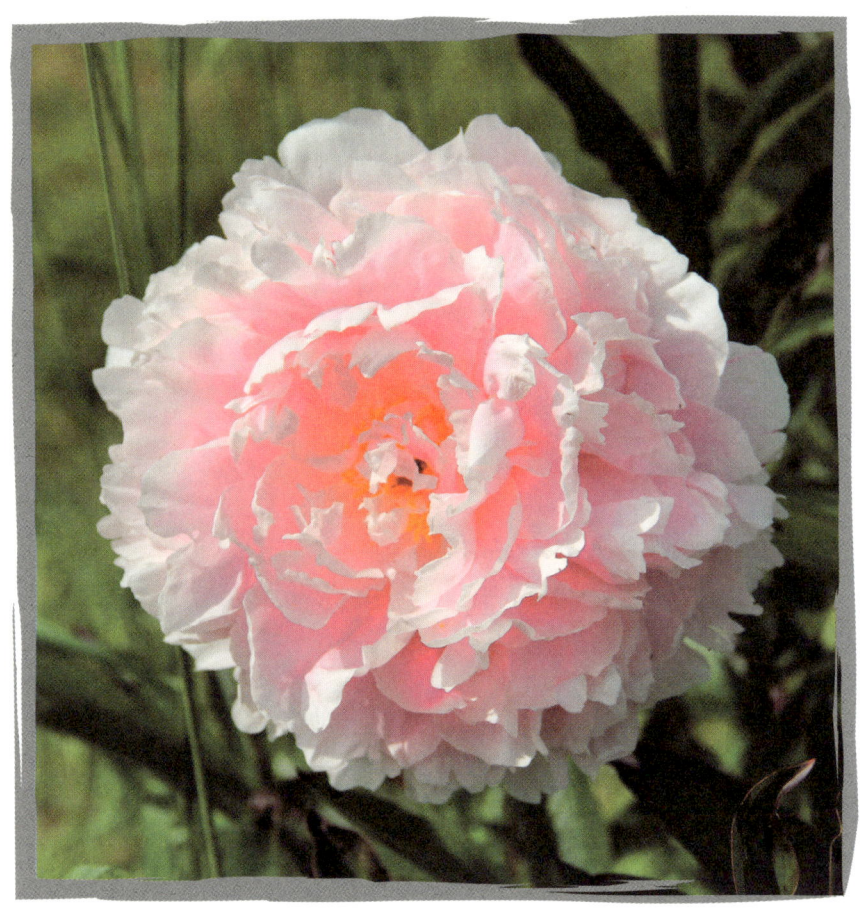

© Kelways Plants Ltd

Sarah Bernhardt

1844–1923

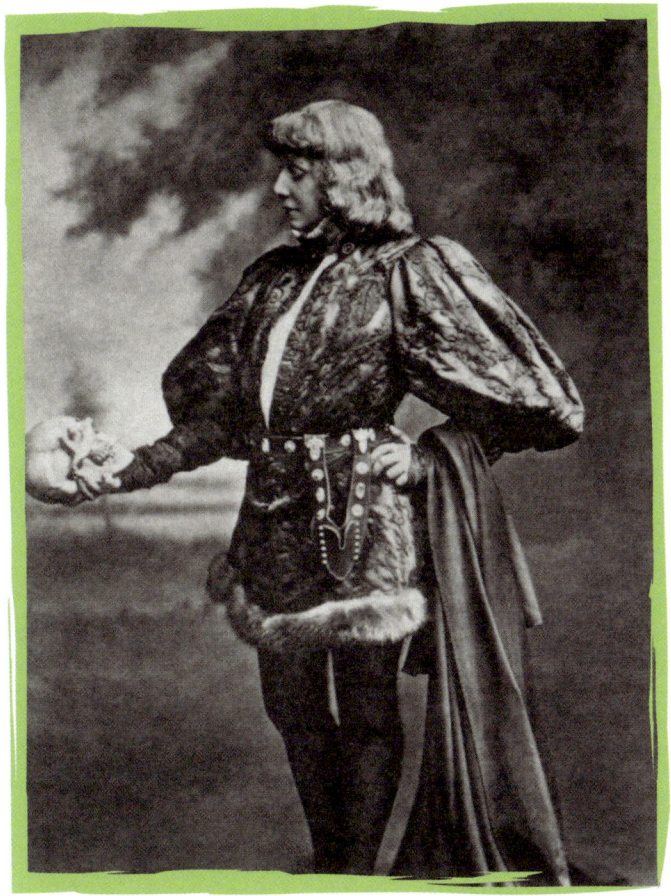

'Alas, poor Yorick!' The lovely Sarah Bernhardt would play
any part in any play to great acclaim, including Hamlet.

HERBACEOUS PEONY
'SARAH BERNHARDT'
IN YOUR GARDEN

'To plant a garden is to believe in tomorrow', said Audrey Hepburn, and the truth of this is confirmed by the hardy herbaceous peony which can reward you with delightful flowers for well over twenty years! So make sure you give it a good start in life.

If you're planting a container-grown plant, choose a sunny spot and dig a hole at least 30cm (12in) deep and wide. Mix in some garden compost and a handful of bonemeal or general fertilizer.

Then – and this is important – avoid planting too deeply. If you have bought it as a containerised plant, it is already potted at the correct level so make sure that you plant to the same depth.

Above all, do not overwater newly planted peonies, as this is the biggest cause of failure. If you are planting in a group, allow about 75cm (30in) between the plants and exercise a little patience – flowering normally starts from the second year after planting.

Kelways Plants Ltd, Picts Hill, Langport, Somerset, TA10 9EZ.
Tel: 01458 250 521. Email: sales@kelways.co.uk www.kelways.co.uk.
See also: The Hardy Plant Society, Peony Group.
www.hardy-plant.org.uk/meet-us-at/specialist-groups/peony.

Sarah Bernhardt

Sarah Henriette Rosine Berhardt grew up knowing a lot about coquetry and sex appeal, because her mother was a courtesan, which meant that she wasn't entirely sure who her father was. The world in which she first saw the light of day was that of the Parisian demi-monde, the haunt of high-class prostitutes, bohemian artists and aristocrats who derived vicarious pleasure from dubious personal contacts with the darker underbelly of French society. One of her mother's sisters, too, was a courtesan, but the other sister, her Aunt Henriette, was a great deal more sensible and took a hand in the upbringing of the young Sarah and her siblings. Sarah was sent away from home to be educated at an Augustine convent outside Versailles but returned to the French capital to study at the Paris Conservatoire in a bid to achieve her dream of becoming an actress. And she did become an actress – quite simply the most famous actress the world, until then, had ever seen.

It wasn't easy at first, though she had an undoubted talent. She joined the repertory company at the Théâtre de l'Odéon, learning her craft in plays by Moliére, Dumas and Victor Hugo. She tackled more significant roles at the Comédie Française, where her most notable success was in Racine's *Phédre*, bringing a new dimension to the title role, to great acclaim.

The company appeared in London during the 1879 season, where audiences fell under her spell and flocked to see her. Outside the theatre, she gave private recitals, became the darling of London society and acquired innumerable admirers who always remained her friends. Among many others, Oscar Wilde was devoted to her, calling her 'the incomparable one' and scattering lilies at her feet.

In time, emboldened by her success, she severed her connections with theatre companies and struck out on her own, visiting America and establishing herself in the part for which she was long remembered – that of Marguerite Gautier in *La Dame aux Camélias*. It was a hugely popular play at the time and many actresses played the tubercular courtesan but none with more success than Berhardt, perhaps because she of all people, drawing on her early experiences among her mother's friends, could really get under the skin of a courtesan.

Now she began behaving like a star and, in America, acquired the satirical nickname of 'Sarah Barnum' because of the circus of publicity which surrounded her. She skilfully manipulated the system to her own advantage and to the delight of her admirers. With immense energy, she travelled the world, visiting London annually. Never idle for a moment, she wrote several books and proved herself to be not only a gifted painter but also a very talented sculptress – twenty-five of her sculptures still exist.

She had love affairs with her leading men and surrounded herself with exotic pets, including monkeys and a cheetah. By the turn of the century she had become an inspiration for women who wanted something more from life than marriage and she was rapidly becoming a national treasure in France. She continued to appear on stage until well into her old age, despite having a leg amputated in 1915. This was because when she appeared on stage in the role of Tosca she habitually threw herself off the parapet in the last act, landing on a mattress behind the scenery, except that on one occasion the mattress was not in position and her badly injured right knee became gangrenous. Astonishingly, the amputation didn't stop her performing and, as late as 1922, when she was 78 years old, she was preparing for a new role and discussing the possibility of making a film.

In 1914, Sarah Bernhardt was made a Chevalier of the Légion d'honneur, the highest French Order of Merit, and she remained indomitable into her old age. Her funeral in 1923 was predictably ostentatious and she lies buried in the Pére Lachaise cemetery in Paris.

HERBACEOUS PEONY
'SHIRLEY TEMPLE'

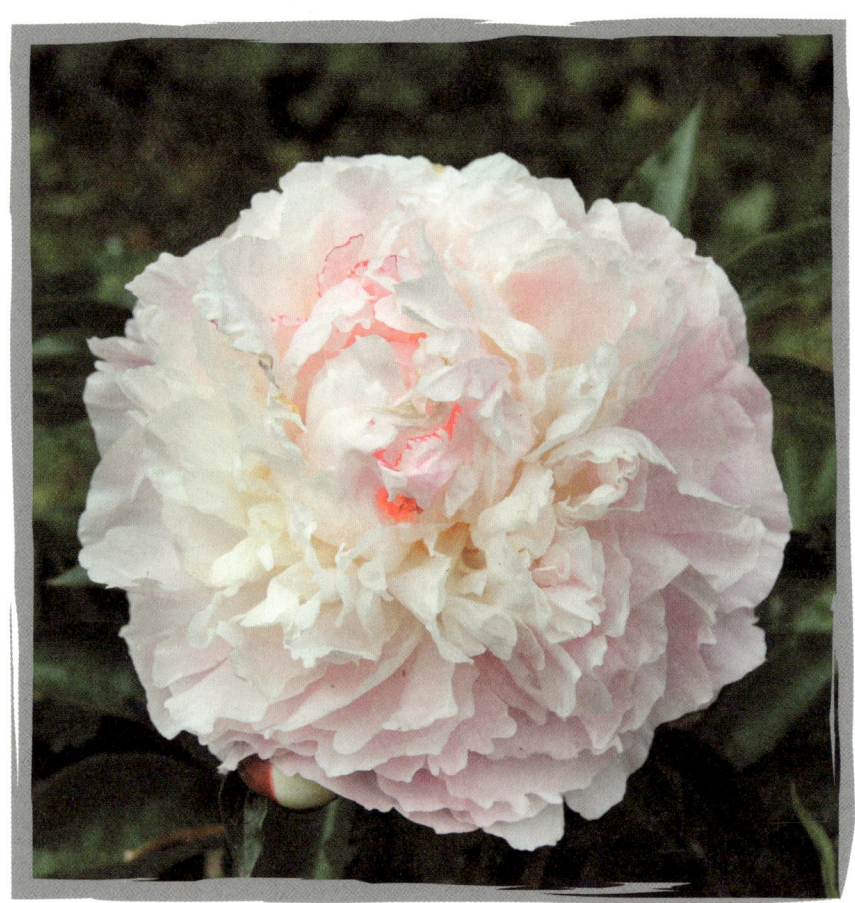

© Kelways Plants Ltd

Shirley Temple

1928-2014

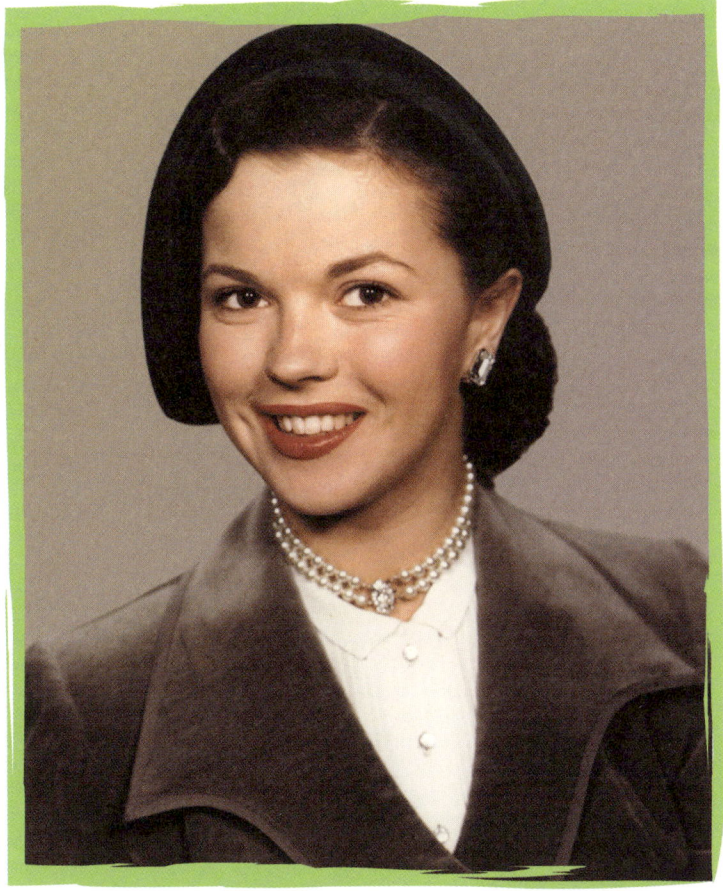

'Thank heaven for little girls', though, of course, they have to grow up. Shirley Temple did so with dignity and, later, great statesmanship.

HERBACEOUS PEONY 'SHIRLEY TEMPLE'

IN YOUR GARDEN

The planting guidelines for 'Sarah Bernhardt' apply equally to 'Shirley Temple' and, once established, both will benefit from a feed with a general fertilizer in the spring, and again in the autumn. Autumn is also the time to remove the dead foliage at ground level and clear it away. If mulching, avoid smothering the top of the crown or the plants may become too deeply buried and stop flowering.

With acidic soils, an occasional top dressing with lime will prove beneficial. After some years, peonies will benefit from being dug up and split in the early autumn, then re-planted. Useful guidelines for this are given on the nursery's website.

Peonies are not bothered by many pests but ants love them because, as the flower buds develop, they exude a sweet, sugary substance. This is a magnet to ants, but don't worry; they will not damage your peony unless they nest within the roots.

Kelways Plants Ltd, Picts Hill, Langport, Somerset, TA10 9EZ.
Tel: 01458 250 521. Email: sales@kelways.co.uk. www.kelways.co.uk.
See also: The Hardy Plant Society, Peony Group.
www.hardy-plant.org.uk/meet-us-at/specialist-groups/peony.

Shirley Temple

'America will be all right...' President Franklin D. Roosevelt once declared, '...as long as we have Shirley Temple.' He was talking about a little girl who was barely ten years old. Shirley Jane Temple, born in Santa Monica in 1928, was the daughter of an ambitious, single-minded mother and a father who worked for the local branch of the Bank of California. With her impish smile and with precisely 56 bouncing curls framing her cherubic face, she was the President's idea of an antidote to the woes of the Great Depression of the 1930s. She had been the dimpled darling of American movie-goers from the age of four.

Shirley Temple was the first – and by far the biggest – child star of the motion picture industry, having been spotted by a casting agent as a three-year-old being taught at 'Miss Meglin's Dance School'. Her very earliest films were short burlesque spoofs of adult features with toddlers in the title roles, often giving rise to salacious responses from the audience but ultimately highlighting the need for stricter censorship. As she grew up and began to star in films precisely tailored to her talents, audiences doted on her. Cute as custard pie, she danced and sang her way through film after film in the 1930s, lisping her lines appealingly in heart-warming scripts about family values and the triumph of good over evil. The youngest ever winner of an Academy Award – she was just seven years old – her wholesome image endorsed merchandise that included sheet music, dolls and dresses and doubled the $1,250 a week already being paid her by Twentieth Century-Fox. 'Moms' across America named countless baby girls after her – Shirley MacLaine was just one of them. As the studio's greatest asset, she was loaned to other studios from time to time, but in 1940 Fox declined to lend her to Metro-Goldwyn-Mayer for *The Wizard of Oz*, so Shirley missed out on the film which made a star of Judy Garland. Nevertheless, Shirley's tally of films is quite astonishing. In all, she starred in fourteen short films, forty-three feature films and over twenty-five 'storybook movies' to huge acclaim.

It was the kind of fame that couldn't last. The little girl had to grow up and Shirley officially retired from films in December 1950. She was just seventeen when she married her first husband, Jack Agar, and their daughter was born shortly afterwards. But the marriage wasn't destined to last – Agar's personal problems led them to divorce after four years and, four years later, Shirley married Charles Black, a former naval officer, becoming known as Shirley Temple Black thereafter.

And it was as Shirley Temple Black that Shirley made a comeback in an entirely different role. She turned to politics and became a prominent member of the Republican Party, gaining high diplomatic office under four presidents. She was appointed US representative to the United Nations under Richard Nixon,

Ambassador to the Republic of Ghana under Gerald Ford, Foreign Affairs officer for the State Department under Ronald Reagan and US ambassador to Czechoslovakia under George W. Bush. She was also the first female Chief of Protocol for the Whitehouse.

In the autumn of 1972, at the age of forty-four, Shirley was diagnosed with breast cancer and successfully underwent surgery. Afterwards, she endeared herself to women throughout America by being prepared to discuss her experience in public, with an article in the magazine *McCall's* and interviews on radio and television programmes. She was, it is claimed, the first person ever to use the words 'cancer' and 'breast' on American television.

Shirley published her autobiography in 1988. Appropriately enough, it's entitled *Child Star.*

SHRUB ROSE
'LADY RYDER OF WARSAW'

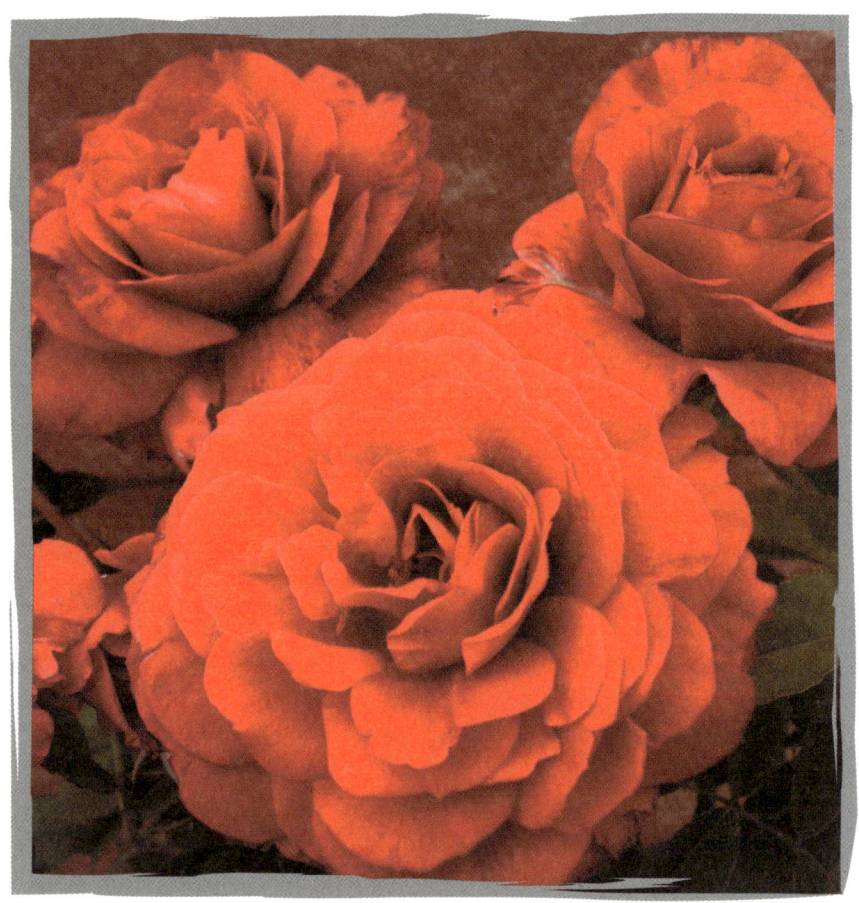

© Harkness Roses

Sue Ryder

1924-2000

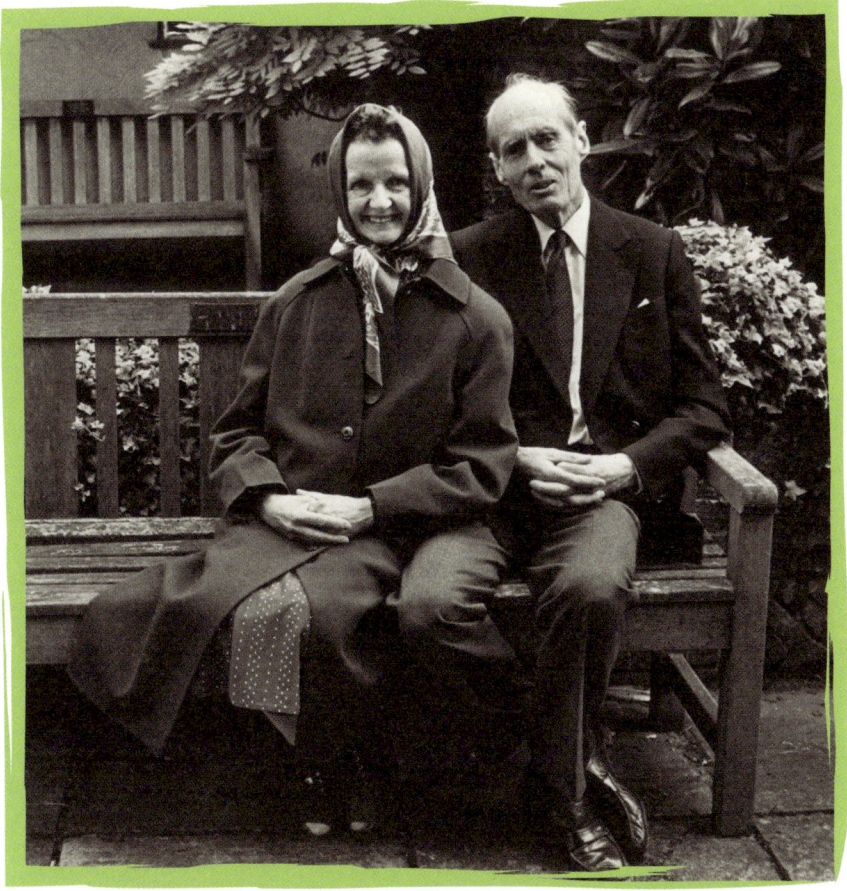

Sue Ryder with her husband, Group Captain Leonard Cheshire VC,
a marriage of kindred spirits forged in Christian commitment.

SHRUB ROSE
'LADY RYDER OF WARSAW'
IN YOUR GARDEN

Members of the Sue Ryder Prayer Fellowship gathered at the 2014 Chelsea Flower Show to see the launch of this delightful double-bloomed shrub rose, because a percentage of its sales go to benefit the work of the Fellowship.

The rose itself is in a rich crimson colour, which remains true even in the strongest sunlight. Small clusters of five or seven flowers, measuring 10cm across (nearly 4in) make a good display against the dense, mid-green foliage throughout the summer.

Though not strongly scented, it has the advantage of a very good disease resistance and the well-branched plant provides plenty of leaf and flower cover, making this an excellent variety to use in beds, borders or hedges.

The mature bush will reach a height of 130cm tall x 90cm wide (approx. 4ft x 3ft). Like many of the more modern varieties, it tends to offer a much longer flowering period and is gratifyingly easy to grow successfully.

Harkness Roses, Cambridge Road, Hitchin, Herts, SG4 0JT.
Tel: 01462 420402. Email: harkness@roses.co.uk. www.roses.co.uk.
See also: The British Association of Rose Breeders. www.rosesuk.com.

Sue Ryder

It is often jokingly said that women tend to lie about their age, but in Sue Ryder's case it was true, though she claimed to be older, not younger, than she really was. Wanting to volunteer for the First Aid Nursing Yeomanry at the outbreak of war in 1939, when she was just fifteen years old, she signed up with a falsified birth date. Oddly, though, the deception endured and she regularly gave her year of birth as 1923, but, according to her official birth and death certificates, Margaret Susan Ryder was actually born a year later, on 3rd July 1924.

There is no record of her having lied at any other time during her life. In fact, she was a woman of the greatest integrity, strongly held religious belief and a genuine desire to help others. She had been influenced by her own mother, who had given generously of her time to do unpaid social work in their home town of Leeds. Here, young Sue was profoundly shocked to see people who had, often through no fault of their own, been driven into poverty in the aftermath of the First World War and forced to live in appalling slum dwellings. With the advent of the Second World War, Sue Ryder knew exactly what she wanted to do and, for the rest of her life, she never wavered from her total commitment to helping others.

Her early wartime experience was in the Polish section of the Special Operations Executive and, when the war came to an end, she volunteered to do relief work, some of which was, again, undertaken in Poland. She came to love the country and its people very deeply. Sue also drove a mobile clinic with the Croix Rouge in northern France and, while in Germany, she recognised that the survivors of concentration camps needed all the available help to get back on their feet again. It was almost history repeating itself. She was briefly able to establish a modest holiday home in Denmark for those whom the war had left with long-term illnesses but she failed to sustain it because of a shortage of funding and returned home to England.

Here, her mother re-enters the story, because she offered her own home in Cavendish, Suffolk, to house the foundation which Sue set up as a residential home for those with physical and mental illnesses. It was funded partly by government and partly from charitable gifts and Sue, who was always aware of the importance of showing gratitude, signed every single letter of acknowledgement of financial help. Eventually, the Sue Ryder Foundation had grown to the point where it ran eighty homes in a dozen countries, including twenty-eight in Poland, as well as a chain of some 500 charity shops.

In 1955, Sue met someone who shared her views and who had also established homes for the disabled. He was Group Captain Leonard Cheshire VC, a war hero, an entirely kindred spirit and, like Sue, a convert to Catholicism. They agreed that they had established their respective homes not with funds but with faith. They married in 1959 and each continued to run their own charitable foundations with the total co-operation of the other. In celebration of their marriage, they also established a joint venture they called the Ryder-Cheshire Foundation. Rightly, this amazing couple garnered many awards and honours in recognition of their charitable work. Sue was awarded the officer's cross of the Order of Polonia Restituta, one of Poland's highest honours, in 1965. She had already been made an OBE in 1957 and became a CMG twenty years later. Then, in 1979, she became a life peer as Baroness Ryder of Warsaw, her title reflecting her life-long devotion to Poland and its people. Membership of the House of Lords gave her the right platform to become a forceful social commentator. In 1991, her husband, too, was created a life peer and took his own seat in the Lords as Baron Cheshire of Woodhall in Lincolnshire. They were among the very few married couples who were each peers in their own right, but the greatest motivation behind this unique partnership was not to seek honour; it was, with all Christian humility, to care for others.

ENGLISH SHRUB ROSE
'SUSAN WILLIAMS-ELLIS'

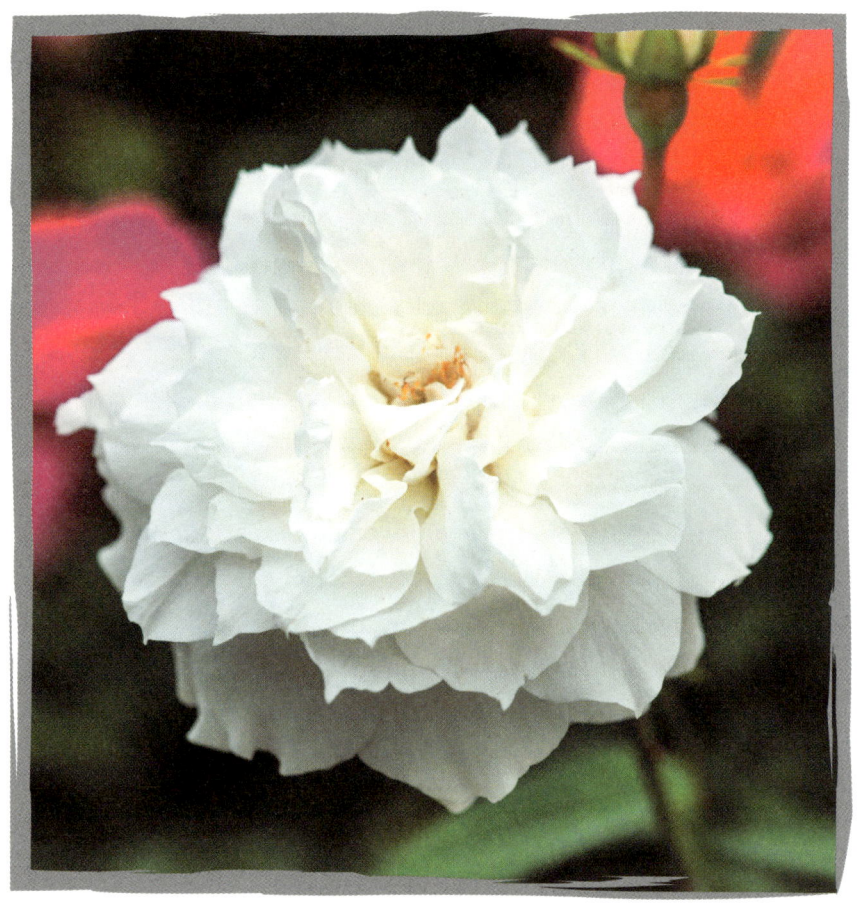

© David Austin Roses

Susan Williams-Ellis

1918–2007

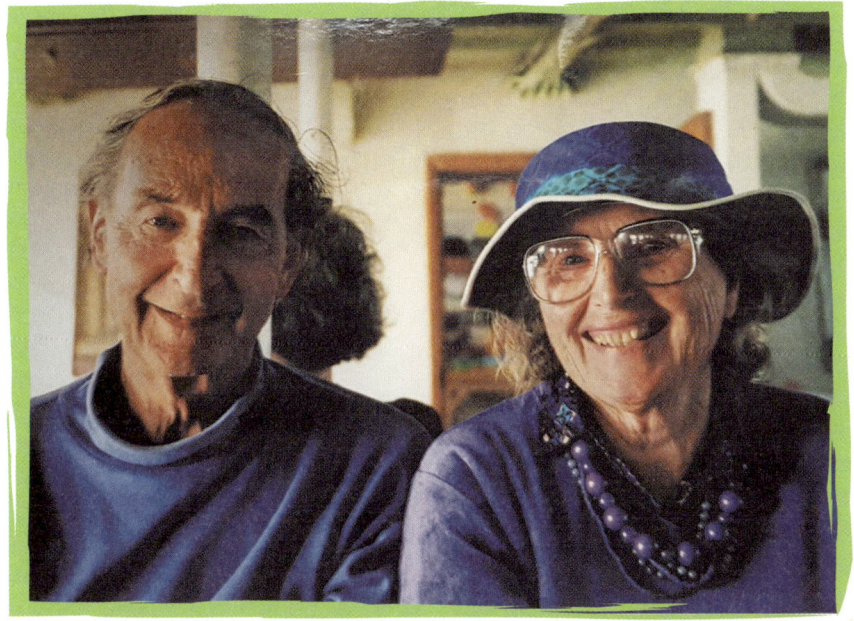

Susan Williams-Ellis in an informal picture with her husband and business partner, Euan Cooper-Willis. By courtesy of the Susan Williams-Ellis Foundation.

ENGLISH SHRUB ROSE
'SUSAN WILLIAMS-ELLIS'
IN YOUR GARDEN

This is always one of the first English shrub roses to flower and continues to do so in repeat flushes over an exceptionally long flowering season, until the first frosts. It is remarkably healthy and extremely winter hardy, with upright, bushy, twiggy growth.

The plant will grace any rose border, grow in all soil types and doesn't mind a small, shady space, or even a large patio pot. It will reward the gardener with a spread of around 120cm (between 3ft and 4ft) of pure white flowers and a strong 'old rose' fragrance.

Generally speaking, the shrub rose is an ideal plant used either singly in a rose border or with other plants in mixed borders. Three or more shrub roses of the same variety planted together will grow to form one dense shrub, which will provide a more continuous display and make a more definite statement in the border.

David Austin Roses, Bowling Green Lane, Albrighton, Wolverhampton, WV7 2HB. Tel: 01902 376 328. Email: help@davidaustinroses.co.uk. www.davidaustinroses.co.uk. See also: The Rose Society UK. www.therosesociety.org.uk.

Susan Williams-Ellis

Though a gifted artist and designer in her own right, Susan Williams-Ellis was probably influenced by her family background. Her parents, the eminent architect Clough Williams-Ellis and his wife, Amabel, numbered well-known artists and writers among their London circle of friends. But Susan, painfully shy, loathed being taken to 'grown-up parties' in Hampstead, attended by the likes of Augustus John and Virginia Woolf. She described the experience as 'horrible!'

In 1934, Susan was accepted as a student at Dartington Hall School in Devon, an international magnet for artists, architects, writers, philosophers and musicians. Here, she studied painting and developed an interest in pottery, which meant that she was already well-grounded in both by the time she entered Chelsea Polytechnic in 1936. The names of her teachers there are the stuff of legend – she learned book illustration from Graham Sutherland and was taught sculpture by Henry Moore. With the advent of WWII, Susan found a crucial outlet for her talents with a job at the Air Ministry, drawing maps for bombing raids.

Tragically, that war robbed her of her brother Christopher, who was killed at Monte Cassino in 1944. Having delayed her wedding while he was 'missing in action', Susan later married Euan Cooper-Willis, the young man who had shared rooms with Christopher at King's College, Cambridge. It must have been a bittersweet occasion for them both. Facing their future together, they couldn't have known that they were destined to put the name of a small Welsh village on the world map.

Susan's father 'Clough', as he was affectionately known, had strong family connections with north Wales and it was here, in 1925, that he began to create what was to become his masterpiece, the village of Portmeirion. A staunch advocate of the establishment of National Parks in England and Wales, he was partly responsible in 1951 for the demarcation of Snowdonia National Park's boundary and, though Portmeirion itself is just south of that boundary, one of the most stunning views of it looks towards the Snowdon mountain range in the background. Rising above the sandy beaches of the Dwyryd Estuary, the village grew between 1925 and 1976 under the influence of Clough's architectural genius. He created some buildings and acquired or adapted others, designing something quite unique that has since been described as being 'full of architectural relics and impish modern fantasies'. Portmeirion, a spectacular Italianate village with sub-tropical gardens in a beautiful setting, is now an outstanding heritage attraction and in great demand as a film location.

In 1953, Clough asked Susan and Euan to take over the management of the gift shop in the village and that's where their enterprise really began. Susan was keen to produce items of souvenir pottery that could be sold in the Portmeirion gift shop and her designs were as practical as they were pleasing.

They proved to be a great success, to the extent that, in 1961, she and Euan were able to acquire a small pottery decorating company in Stoke-on-Trent and a pottery manufacturing company the following year. They combined the two, thereby creating Portmeirion Potteries Ltd. It seemed that Susan had hit upon a magic formula for producing useful, everyday items that were objects of beauty in themselves. One of the first was the popular cylindrical shape of the tall, straight coffee pot embossed with her 'Totem' design, repeated in other colours and other items in the same range. Then, in 1972, a range of tableware was produced which proved to be the most enduringly popular of all Susan's designs. This was the highly regarded 'Botanic Garden', largely based on nineteenth-century illustrations from Thomas Green's *The Universal Herbal* and Rebecca Hey's *The Moral of Flowers*. The range soon accounted for nearly half the company's sales and enabled the expansion of the factory to fuel the demand for it. By 1988, Portmeirion Potteries was exporting to no less than thirty-four countries and had been floated on the Stock Exchange. In 2002, Susan was awarded an honorary degree by the University of Keele for her outstanding contribution to the ceramics industry. She died at her home in north Wales in November 2007.

GLADIOLUS 'VERA LYNN'

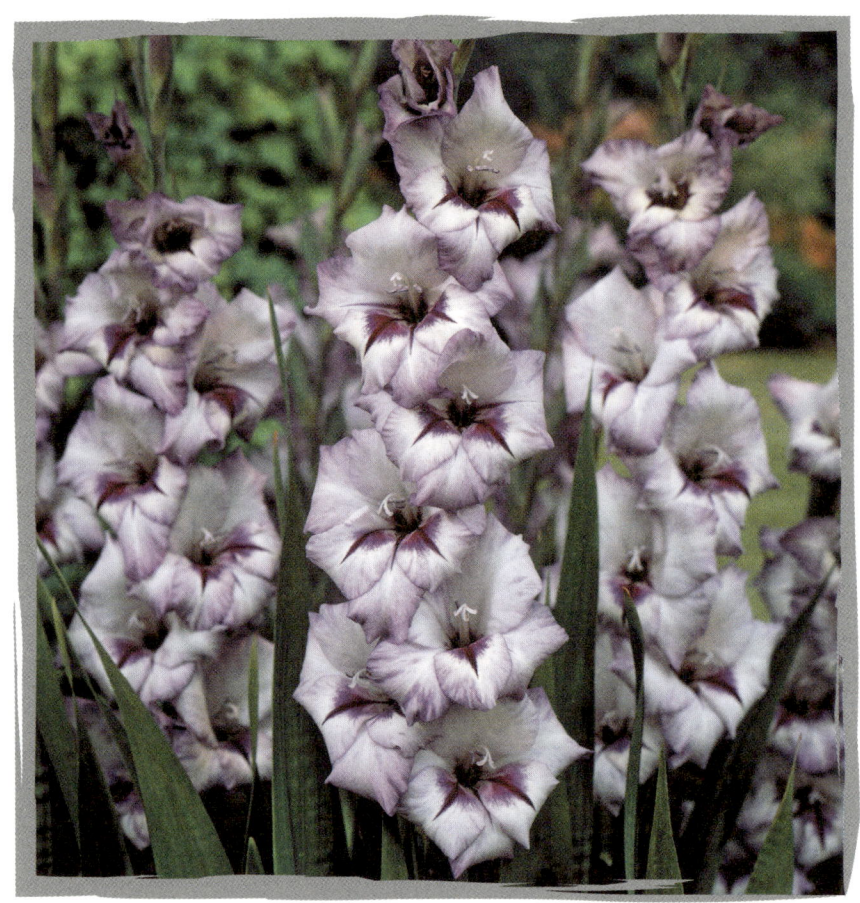

© visionspictures

Vera Lynn

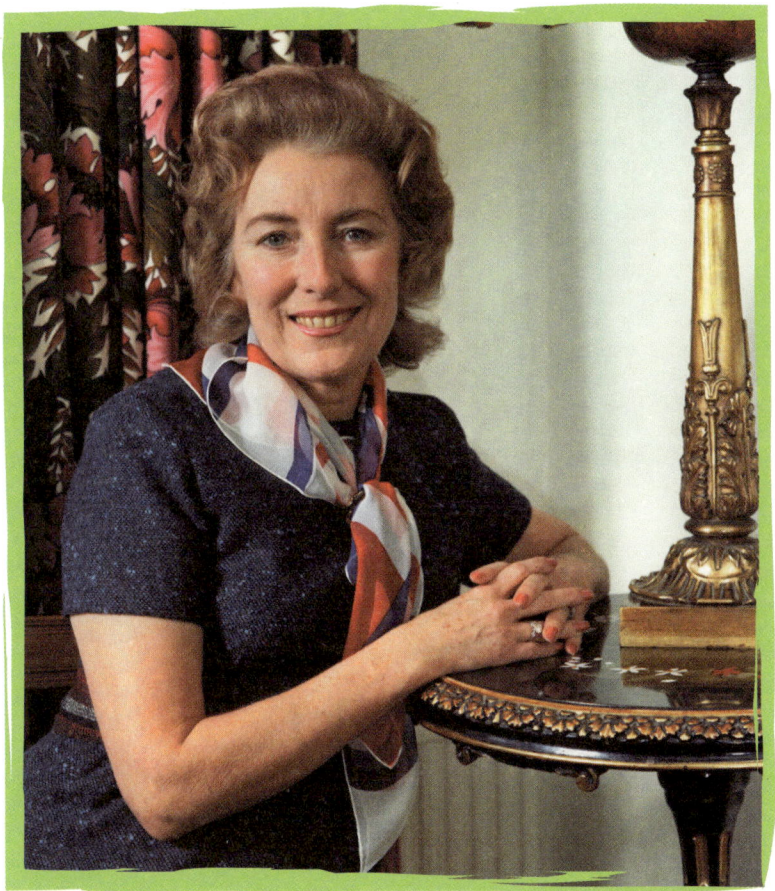

Vera Lynn, the nostalgic voice of home for so many serving men and women in WWII, seen here in a portrait by Allan Warren, 1973.

GLADIOLUS 'VERA LYNN'
IN YOUR GARDEN

A wonderfully old-fashioned flower which is slowly but surely becoming fashionable once more, Gladioli are cormous perennials of the iris family. Their name derives from the Latin word for 'a sword'. This is why they are sometimes appropriately known as 'sword lilies', since their funnel-shaped flowers are set against sword-shaped leaves. Quite often, though, they are affectionately just known as 'glads' or 'gladdies' in the more traditional cottage garden.

This one makes a very valuable addition to the modern flower border with lovely blooms of soft blue, having a splodge of pure purple at the throat. They're also really good for cutting, lasting for well over a week in the vase.

The plants themselves are easy to grow and to care for, given a well-drained soil in a sunny border. The corms should be planted to a depth of 1ocm (3.5in) and they will grow to a height of 90cm (3ft).

After the growing season, mature plants can be easily propagated by division, that is by lifting and separating the cormlets when dormant, ready for repeating the cycle again the following year.

Mr. Fothergill's Seeds Ltd, Gazeley Road, Kentford, Suffolk, CB8 7QB.
Tel: 01638 751 161. www.mr-fothergills.co.uk.
See also: The British Gladiolus Society. www.britglad.com.

Vera Lynn

There is no question that Dame Vera Lynn can lay claim to being one of Britain's foremost 'national treasures', because this was the young woman whose distinctive voice sang songs for heroes throughout the Second World War.

Vera Margaret Welch was born in modest circumstances at East Ham, in what is now the London borough of Newham, in March 1917. A talented little singer from an early age, she was performing locally at the age of seven. Then, clearly determined to turn her talent into a professional career, at the age of eleven she began using the maiden name of her maternal grandmother, Margaret Lynn, as her own stage name. From then on, she was never anything other than Vera Lynn but she couldn't possibly have dreamed of how well known and well loved that name would become throughout the English-speaking world.

1935 saw Vera's first-ever radio broadcast with the Joe Loss Orchestra and she made an instant impact. Soon she was recording and broadcasting not only with Joe Loss but with several other famous bands and in 1937 she signed up with the best-known band of the era under bandleader Bert Ambrose. With the outbreak of war in 1939, Vera Lynn recorded her first major hit, which was absolutely in tune with the times. As countless young men were leaving wives and sweethearts to go abroad to fight for their country, Vera recorded the song

We'll Meet Again. With powerfully hopeful lyrics and a memorable melody, it resonated with service personnel and their families and was without doubt the biggest hit of the war years. She followed it with other titles, including *The White Cliffs of Dover, There'll Always Be an England* and *A Nightingale Sang in Berkeley Square.* These were the tunes which were hummed, strummed and whistled throughout the war.

Vera's huge wartime popularity arose from two things: one was her own radio programme, *Sincerely Yours,* in which she sang popular songs and relayed messages to British troops overseas from their families at home. She visited hospitals and recorded messages from new mothers to the fathers of their babies, who were serving abroad.

Perhaps most importantly, Vera Lynn wasn't frightened by the prospect of going into war zones herself, to sing for the servicemen and women. She joined the Entertainments National Service Association (ENSA) and toured Egypt and India, giving outdoor concerts for the troops, often on makeshift stages. Notably, she entertained British guerilla units in Japanese-occupied Burma and, in recognition of her courage and her contribution to the morale of the troops, she was later awarded the famous military campaign medal, the Burma Star.

During the war years, Vera had married fellow musician Harry Lewis, whom she met when they both worked with the Bert

Ambrose Orchestra; Harry was a clarinettist in the band. After the war was over, the devoted couple moved to north London, where they brought up their daughter and lived like any normal family. Now with Harry as her manager, Vera continued to record and had a remarkable three singles in the first-ever singles chart. She was enormously popular on radio, had her own series on BBC1 in the 1950s and 1960s and was a frequent guest on other programmes. Her recorded output was quite staggering – she recorded album after album over many years and had the distinction of being the oldest recording artist in the world when a compilation of her greatest hits was released to mark her 100th birthday in 2017. It reached number three in the charts!

Not surprisingly, Vera Lynn garnered many honours during her long life, including that of Dame Commander of the Order of the British Empire. Less well known is that several of those honours were for her behind-the-scenes charity work, which had benefitted ex-servicemen, disabled children and the Breast Cancer Research Trust. But, of all her many titles, the one which will always be most warmly associated with her is that of British Forces' Sweetheart.

THE NAMING OF PLANTS
ROYAL HORTICULTURAL SOCIETY

Probably the most exquisite, lasting compliment anyone can
be paid is to have a flower named in their honour. And, though
Pretty Maids celebrates the lives and achievements of women,
you can choose to name a flower after anyone, male or female,
whom you admire or admired during their lifetime. Flowers are
often named for men, for example, the distinguished breeder
David Austin has developed, among many others, a climbing
rose named for the virtuoso flautist James Galway and a shrub
rose which commemorates the much-loved children's writer
Roald Dahl. So, yes, it is possible to have a flower named in
celebration of the life or work of a loved one, a friend, relative or
colleague and this would be a particularly suitable tribute if he
or she loved gardening or took delight in the beauty of flowers.

So how do you set about doing this? Quite simply, the best
advice is to be found on the website of the UK's foremost
gardening charity, the Royal Horticultural Society but, before
you make any decisions, you should consider a few important
points, including the fact that it is often neither quick nor easy
to have a plant named in this way.

The first thing to do is to think about which type of flower
would best suit the person you want to commemorate. Should
you choose a rose, perhaps? Or did that person have a favourite
flower? A dahlia? A fuchsia? A clematis? Once you've made your
choice, you should find out if there is a registrar who oversees

the naming of flowers for the particular genus you have in mind. To do this, you can consult the register maintained by the International Society for Horticultural Science, whose contact details appear on page 199 in the Useful Contacts list. If there is a registrar for the plant of your choice, then you should be able to find out if they are able to refer you to any breeders who may offer this service. Of course, breeders have to make a living, so do be aware that they are likely to make a charge for plant naming and this can be quite expensive. If there isn't a register and you are unable to find a breeder to help, then try approaching a nursery which specialises in that plant to ask their advice.

But pause for a moment because there are other ways of ensuring that someone's name is remembered. For example, rather than a flower, you could pay a lasting tribute by planting a tree or a shrub in that person's name. If you haven't got room in your own garden for this or you would like a more public memorial, perhaps your local park has a scheme which would work well for you. There are civic gardens, too, which would be pleased to receive a shrub or a sapling as a gift from you and they might even be happy to arrange for a small commemorative plaque to be erected nearby. The Woodland Trust and the National Forest are also two organisations that can arrange a planting in memory of a loved one, so there's no need to spend a lot of money in order to achieve a beautiful, living memorial.

As you leaf through this book, you'll realise that by far the most popular flower chosen for remembrance is the rose and professional organisations and societies will often commission growers to create a new variety to bear the name of their founder or the person most associated with them – think of the roses named for Dr. Elizabeth Casson, for example, or for Emily Brontë. It is possible for individuals to enter into an agreement with a breeder, but be warned: this could prove a prohibitively expensive option. Rose breeding is a highly skilled and time-consuming undertaking and the cost of breeding an entirely new rose that is vigorous enough to be sold commercially could cost anything between £2,000 and £10,000 or even more. Given that you decide to go ahead, the British Association of Rose Breeders will advise you on how best to set about achieving your aims.

If your heart is absolutely set on naming a rose but you don't want to spend a great deal of money and you only want to share your memories privately with friends and family, then you would be wise to go down the amateur road, rather than choose the professional route. If you make contact with the Amateur Rose Breeders Association, they might be able to help you arrange the naming of a rose which will be attractive and unique but may not have shown the promise to become a commercial variety. It can't therefore be supplied to garden centres or nurseries and, unless propagated from cuttings, there is always the risk that it will be lost to cultivation. The cost for naming such a rose is likely to be around £50 but could be as much as several hundred pounds. If you decide that this is the option for you, then there are several companies and organisations which advertise this service and their names appear below.

More details of this and all other RHS schemes and services are explained in detail on the society's website: www.rhs.org.uk.

SOME USEFUL CONTACTS:

(Please note that the mention of any supplier or service given here does not necessarily constitute an endorsement by the Royal Horticultural Society.)

- The International Society for Horticultural Science: www.ishs.org

- The Woodland Trust: www.woodlandtrust.org.uk

- The National Forest: www.nationalforest.org

- The British Association of Rose Breeders: www.rosesuk.com

- The Amateur Rose Breeders' Association: www.arba.org.uk

- World of Roses: www.rosesuk.com

- Country Garden Roses: www.countrygardenroses.co.uk

- Rose Names: www.rosenames.co.uk

Mari Griffith

1940–2019

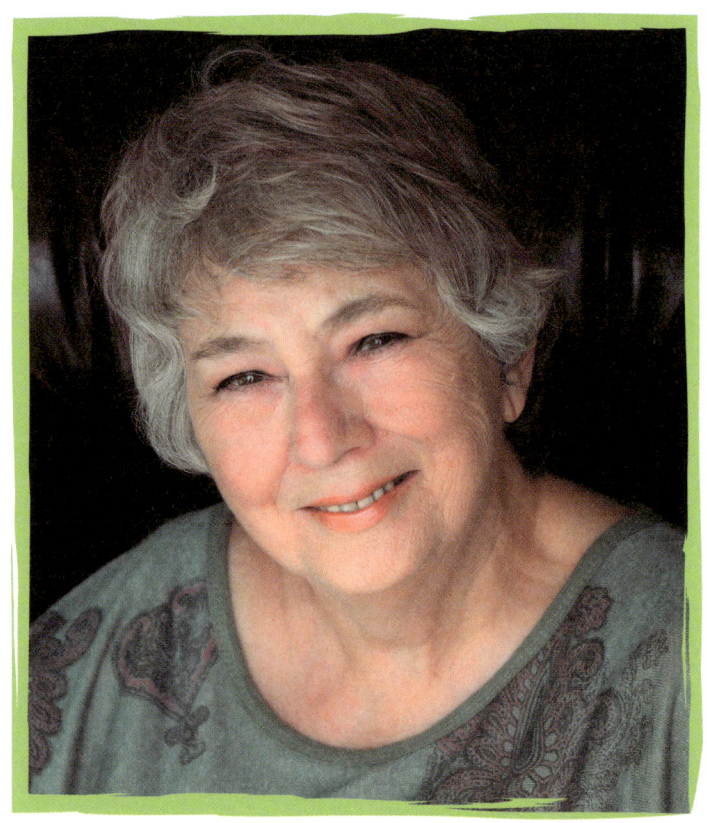

Mari Griffith described herself as a 'recent convert' to gardening, having limited time as a hobby during her busy career in broadcasting. She began as a freelance musician, singing to her own guitar accompaniment, and became well known in the 1970s as a presenter of programmes for BBC Schools Music service and more sophisticated fare for adult audiences both on radio and television. A change of direction saw her take up a variety of staff jobs with the BBC, initially as a continuity announcer, then, after intensive training, as a television director and producer. Mari turned to writing historical novels in her retirement and her first novel, *Root of the Tudor Rose*, became an Amazon bestseller. *The Witch of Eye* followed, the story behind the most sensational treason trial of the 15th century. *Pretty Maids* is Mari's non-fiction debut and final book.

Sadly, Mari was diagnosed with cancer whilst writing *Pretty Maids* and was unwell whilst researching and preparing the book for publication. Mari won the race to finish the work, but subsequently died on Monday 13 May 2019 in Y Bwthyn Newydd, the hospice run by The Princess of Wales Hospital, Bridgend. Mari had wanted the book to be published in time for the Chelsea Flower Show in May, but her illness delayed publication, which followed later in 2019. As Mari had wished, all royalties are to be donated to The Caron Keating Foundation, The Marie Curie Foundation and to Macmillan Cancer Support.

www.marigriffith.co.uk

USEFUL INFORMATION

1. Adelina Patti

Crais-y-Nos Castle, Adelina Patti's beautiful hideaway home in Wales is now a spectacular venue for holidays – or a romantic wedding. www.craigynoscastle.com.

2. Beryl Reid

This book gives us an affectionate and comprehensive account of Beryl Reid's life: *Roll out the Beryl: The Authorised biography of Beryl Reid* by Kaye Crawford (Fantom Films Limited, 2016).

3. Caron Keating

The Caron Keating Foundation specialises in helping small but significant cancer charities, professional carers and support groups.

The Caron Keating Foundation (Registered Charity 1106160) www.caronkeating.org.

Gloria's honest accounts of her experiences are also well documented in her books:

- *Next to You* (Penguin, 2006).
- *Always With You* (Hodder & Stoughton, 2009).
- *Gloria Hunniford: My Life – The Autobiography* (John Blake, 2007).

4. Constance Spry

Copies of Constance Spry's flower arrangements appear online on specialist websites. There's more information about her in the biography *The Surprising Life of Constance Spry* by Sue Shephard (MacMillan, 2010).

Most of her own dozen or so books are no longer available but her classic, written with her colleague Rosemary Hume, has never been out of print: *The Constance Spry Cookery Book* (Dent, 1956).

5. Elizabeth Casson

The Elizabeth Casson Trust, formed in 1948, aims to support the furtherance of Occupational Therapy and its charitable purpose is to advance the profession of Occupational Therapy through research, education and the development of occupational therapists.

The Elizabeth Casson Trust, (Registered Charity 227166) www.elizabethcassontrust.org.uk

The Elizabeth Casson Trust Dorset House Archive is held at RADAR, the Research Archive and Digital Asset Repository at Oxford Brookes University, Headington Campus. www.brookes.ac.uk.

6. Elizabeth Fry

Elizabeth Fry's history is well documented online and elsewhere. Her passion for penal reform lives on in the charity:
The Howard League for Penal Reform (Registered Charity 251926) www.howardleague.org.

7. Ellen Willmott

Ellen's garden at Warley Place is now a 25-acre nature reserve and welcomes visitors – the best time to visit is in the springtime. You'll find it on the B186 (Brentwood to South Ockendon), just south of Brentwood in Essex. Map reference TQ 583 906. Warley Place is run by
The Essex Wildlife Trust, (Registered Charity 210065), www.essexwt.org.uk/reserves/warley-place.

8. Lady Emma Hamilton

The National Portrait Gallery in London lists 35 portraits of Emma Hamilton by various painters, though not all are on display. www.npg.org.uk.

The gallery is within a stone's throw of the landmark 'Nelson's Column' in London's Trafalgar Square.

9. Emily Brontë

The Brontë family home at Haworth in West Yorkshire, where the sisters wrote their books is now a museum and home to the Brontë Society, one of the oldest literary societies in the world. You'll find full details of how and when to visit on their comprehensive website:
Bronte Parsonage Museum,
Registered Charity 529952
www.bronte.org.uk

10. Gertrude Jekyll

Gertrude Jekyll designed and created some 400 gardens and you can find details of those which you can still visit, together with a list of her books, on the official website:
www.gertrudejekyll.co.uk

Godalming Museum in Surrey also has many of her notebooks and copies of all her garden drawings:
www.godalmingmuseum.org.uk.

11. Gloriana

The first representation of Queen Elizabeth I as 'Gloriana' is in the church of St. Faith's in Bacton, Herefordshire, housed in a memorial niche for the Queen's Chief Gentlewoman, Blanche Parry. There is a great deal more about their relationship in this book:
Mistress Blanche: Queen Elizabeth I's Confidante by Ruth E. Richardson (Logaston Press, 2nd edition 2018).

You can also visit St. Faith's Church and download this informative guide to its history – again written by Ruth E. Richardson.
www.blancheparry.co.uk.

You'll find some stunning pictures of the royal row barge *Gloriana* on the charity's website: The Gloriana Trust Charity No: 1160986
www.glorianaqrb.org.uk

12. Grace Kelly

There are reams of information about Grace Kelly on the internet. Less information is given about her charitable activities but you might like to check out the World Association of Children's Friends at www.amade-mondiale.org and The Princess Grace Foundation-USA, www.pgfusa.org.

13. Jacqueline du Pré

The best way to appreciate the genius of Jacqueline du Pré is to listen to recordings of her performances. The following are considered among her finest:

- Elgar Cello concerto with the London Symphony Orchestra conducted by Sir John Barbirolli.
- Brahms Cello Sonatas Nos. 1 & 2, accompanied by Daniel Barenboim.

14. Lady Boothby

Fonmon Castle, Lady Boothby's historic home in the Vale of Glamorgan, changed hands in early 2019 for only the second time in 800 years, having been owned by just two families since the year 1180. In later years it had been used as a venue to host prestigious corporate events and weddings – this is to continue under the new owners.
www.fonmoncastle.com

15. Lady Isobel Barnett

After her long association with the panel game *What's My Line?*, Lady Isobel Barnett published her autobiography wittily entitled *My Life Line* (Hutchinson & Co., 1956).

It is no longer in print but you might be lucky enough to pick up a second-hand copy.

You will find an abundance of information on growing hostas in the definitive work on the subject: *The New Encylopedia of Hostas* by Diana Grenfell, illustrated by Michael Shadrack. (Timber Press. Revised edition 2010).

16. Lucy Locket

The origin of nursery rhymes is fascinating. There are excellent books on the subject, including: *The Oxford Dictionary of Nursery Rhymes* by Iona and Peter Opie, illustrated by Joan Hassall (Oxford University Press, 1963. Revised edition 1997); and *Pop Goes the Weasel: The Secret Meanings of Nursery Rhymes* by Albert Jack (Penguin, 2008).

17. Madam Speaker

The Speaker is the chief officer and highest authority of the House of Commons, a position which dates back to 1377. Since the Speaker also represents the Commons to the monarch, the role has sometimes been quite perilous and seven Speakers were beheaded between 1394 and 1535. You can find further fascinating facts about the way in which the UK is governed on the website www.parliament.uk.

18. Marie Curie

The Marie Curie charity runs nine hospices throughout the UK but also offers care and counselling to those in the wider community who are living with a terminal illness. Their informative, helpful website will tell you more:

Marie Curie, Registered Charity 207994 – England and Wales SC038731 – Scotland www.mariecurie.org.uk

19. Natasha Richardson

Natasha Richardson had the compassion to see beyond the glare of the footlights and worked tirelessly for The National Aids Trust (www.nat.org.uk) and the American Foundation for AIDS Research (www.amfar.org).

20. Nell Gwynn

The only statue of Nell Gwynn (with a Cavalier King Charles spaniel at her feet), is over the entrance to a block of serviced apartments in London's Sloan Avenue – and you can stay there if you wish: www.nellgwynnchelsea.london.

21. Nellie Melba

Like Adelina Patti, Nellie Melba's early gramophone recordings give us little or no idea of how she really sounded, but her own account of an early recording session makes interesting reading. You can find the full transcript on the Melba Museum's website (www. nelliemelbamuseum.com.au). How different recording techniques are now!

22. Nora Barlow

Not surprisingly, several of the descendants of Charles Darwin have written about their distinguished family. Among them are the poet Ruth Padel, who celebrates the life of her famous ancestor in a highly acclaimed anthology: *Darwin: A Life in Poems* by Ruth Padel (Chatto & Windus, 2009).

She also recalls her grandmother Nora Barlow on her own website: www.ruthpadel.com/article/aquilegia-nora-barlow.

Another of Darwin's great-great-granddaughters, the novelist Emma Darwin, celebrates the whole family in her book *This is Not a Book About Charles Darwin: A writer's journey through my family* (Holland House Books, 2019).

23. Octavia Hill

More than a hundred years after her death, Octavia Hill's legacy lives on and her ideas and ideals are celebrated by the Octavia Hill Society. Its aims and its work are well-documented in the website: The Octavia Hill Birthplace Museum Trust, Registered Charity 1018947, www.octaviahill.org.

More well known is the nationwide charitable organisation of which she was one of the founders and which, to this day, ensures environmental and heritage conservation in the UK, the National Trust: www.nationaltrust.org.uk.

24. Odette

Odette herself describes her wartime ordeals in an astonishing interview with Mavis Nicholson on Thames Television's *Afternoon Plus* programme in 1980. You can see it on YouTube by following this link: bit.ly/2G9lUi8.

25. Rosamund Clifford

Fair Rosamund and King Henry's trysting place was at the palace of Woodstock, near Oxford, on the site where Blenheim Palace now stands; the ruins of Godstow Priory are only a few miles away. There's little sign of Rosamund there now, but Blenheim Palace has a rich history of its own: www.blenheimpalace.com.

26. Sarah Bernhardt

Despite the fact that, at the time of her funeral in 1923, film was still in its comparative infancy, there is quite astonishing silent film footage of her funeral procession in Paris and the great outpouring of grief at her death. It clearly shows her effect on her public: bit.ly/2BNtGKq.

27. Shirley Temple

There's a wealth of photographs and other memorabilia online in the official website for Shirley Temple, home of America's Little Darling: www.shirleytemple.com.

28. Sue Ryder

The Sue Ryder charity perpetuates its founder's name in its work to support people through the most difficult times of their lives. It offers palliative, neurological and bereavement support with compassion and expert care.

Sue Ryder Charity
Registered Charity 1052076 in England and Wales
SC039578 in Scotland
www.sueryder.org

The Lady Ryder of Warsaw Memorial Trust was set up by Baroness Ryder of Warsaw CMG OBE shortly before her death in 2000 so that her good works could continue. www.lrwmt.org.uk.

29. Susan Williams-Ellis

The name of Susan Williams-Ellis will always be associated with the village of Portmeirion in north Wales and with her ceramic designs that take the name of the village. There is nowhere quite like Portmeirion and you can experience the magic for yourself, either as a day visitor or a guest, at the Portmeirion Hotel. Full details for all options are on the website for the village: www.portmeirion.wales.

Equally comprehensive is the pottery's dedicated web site at: www.portmeirion.co.uk.

30. Vera Lynn

Dame Vera is proud to be President of the charity to which she has given her name. In 1953, she was one of the founders of The Stars Organisation for Spastics (as it was then called), which started her link to children with cerebral palsy. Her support and commitment culminated in the establishment of the Dame Vera Lynn Children's Charity, which supports and enables children under five with cerebral palsy and other motor learning impairments to reach their full potential. She has devoted much of her time to it since its inception in 2001.

Dame Vera Lynn Children's Charity
Registered Charity 1089657
dvlcc.org.uk

ACKNOWLEDGEMENTS

Researching this book has been a great joy and has given me a legitimate excuse to approach many wonderful people who would otherwise have remained just names to me. They were all, without exception, keen to help. Big thanks, then, go to Alan Titchmarsh and to Rae Spencer-Jones and her colleagues at the Royal Horticultural Society for their involvement. I'm particularly grateful to individual growers and nurseries for providing me with pictures of their flowers and, since I undertook to compile brief horticultural tips based on information which appears on their websites, I alone am responsible for any misinterpretations! If only for that reason, I urge readers to visit those websites in order to get the best out of their flowers.

Various charities and societies associated with the featured 'maids' were especially helpful and I sincerely hope that they will all benefit to some extent from the publicity which this book might afford them. In writing the biographies, I made extensive use of the internet, of course, but I was also careful to check the veracity of my pen-portraits. For this I referred to that most trustworthy of sources, *The Oxford Dictionary of National Biography*. Its riches are freely available to members of subscribing local libraries and I am grateful to the Vale of Glamorgan Libraries service for facilitating my research.

Pretty Maids has plodded a lengthy path to publication and I'm pleased that a suggestion from my dear friend Wendy Gruffydd finally guided it towards the home straight.

Mari Griffith

PHOTO CREDITS

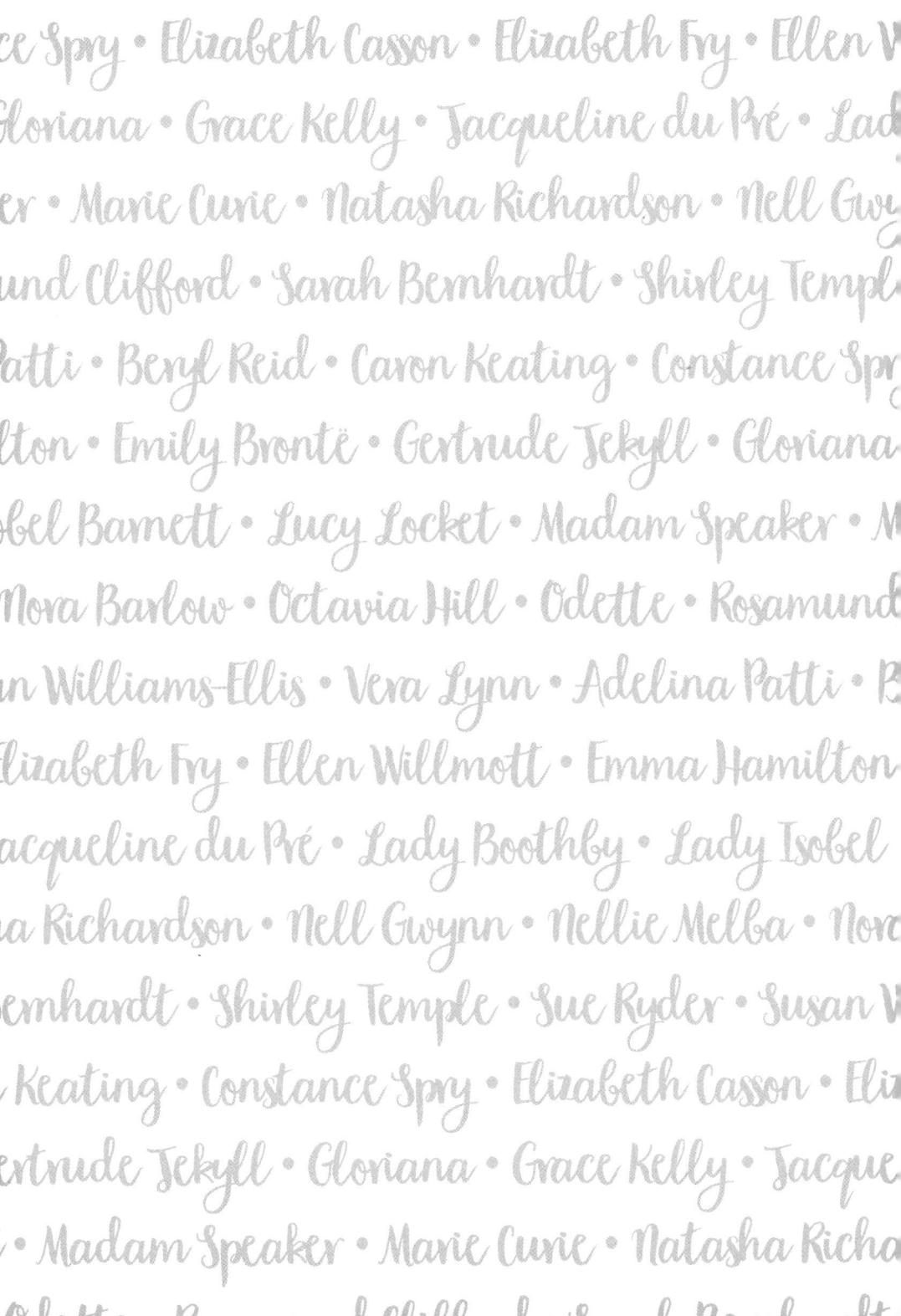

Adelina Patti • Beryl Reid • Caron Keating • Cons
Emma Hamilton • Emily Brontë • Gertrude Jekyl
• Lady Isobel Barnett • Lucy Locket • Madam Sp
Melba • Nora Barlow • Octavia Hill • Odette • Ros
Ryder • Susan Williams-Ellis • Vera Lynn • Adeli
Casson • Elizabeth Fry • Ellen Willmott • Emma He
Kelly • Jacqueline du Pré • Lady Boothby • Lad
• Natasha Richardson • Nell Gwynn • Nellie Melb
Sarah Bernhardt • Shirley Temple • Sue Ryder •
• Caron Keating • Constance Spry • Elizabeth Casso
Brontë • Gertrude Jekyll • Gloriana • Grace Kelly
Lucy Locket • Madam Speaker • Marie Curie • Na
Octavia Hill • Odette • Rosamund Clifford • Sara
Ellis • Vera Lynn • Adelina Patti • Beryl Reid • C
Ellen Willmott • Emma Hamilton • Emily Brontë
• Lady Boothby • Lady Isobel Barnett • Lucy Lo